Tucker Randolph's smart, perceptive, and lengthy letters and diary entries supply vivid insight into the war in Virginia. He wrote valuable narratives on Romney and Kernstown, but the book's best content prints Randolph's accounts of Spotsylvania. They are among the very best primary documents anywhere on that crucial fortnight in 1864.

- Robert K. Krick, author of *Stonewall Jackson at Cedar Mountain*

A feast for the social historian, Tucker Randolph's letters and diaries are alight with evidence of class privilege, the leveling hardships of soldiering, and vibrant material culture. While the scope of Tucker's service was grand, from private to staff officer in both the eastern and western theaters, this is the best account of the storied 21st Virginia Infantry's early days. Peter C. Luebke edits with an intelligent and respectful regard for the source material, providing rich historical context at satisfying moments and immersing us in Randolph's world.

- Kathryn Shively, author of *Nature's Civil War*

St. Joseph Tucker Randolph's wartime diaries and letters take readers from the war's earliest fights in western Virginia to the hard-fought Overland Campaign where he met his end. Ably edited by Peter C. Luebke, Randolph's writings vividly convey war's uncertainty while painfully relating the conflict's impact upon the land and its people. *From Western Virginia with Jackson to Spotsylvania with Lee* is a welcome addition to the rich body of firsthand accounts from the Civil War era thanks to Randolph's insightful observations and breadth of wartime experiences.

- Dr. James J. Broomall, Director
George Tyler Moore Center for the Study of the Civil War
Shepherd University

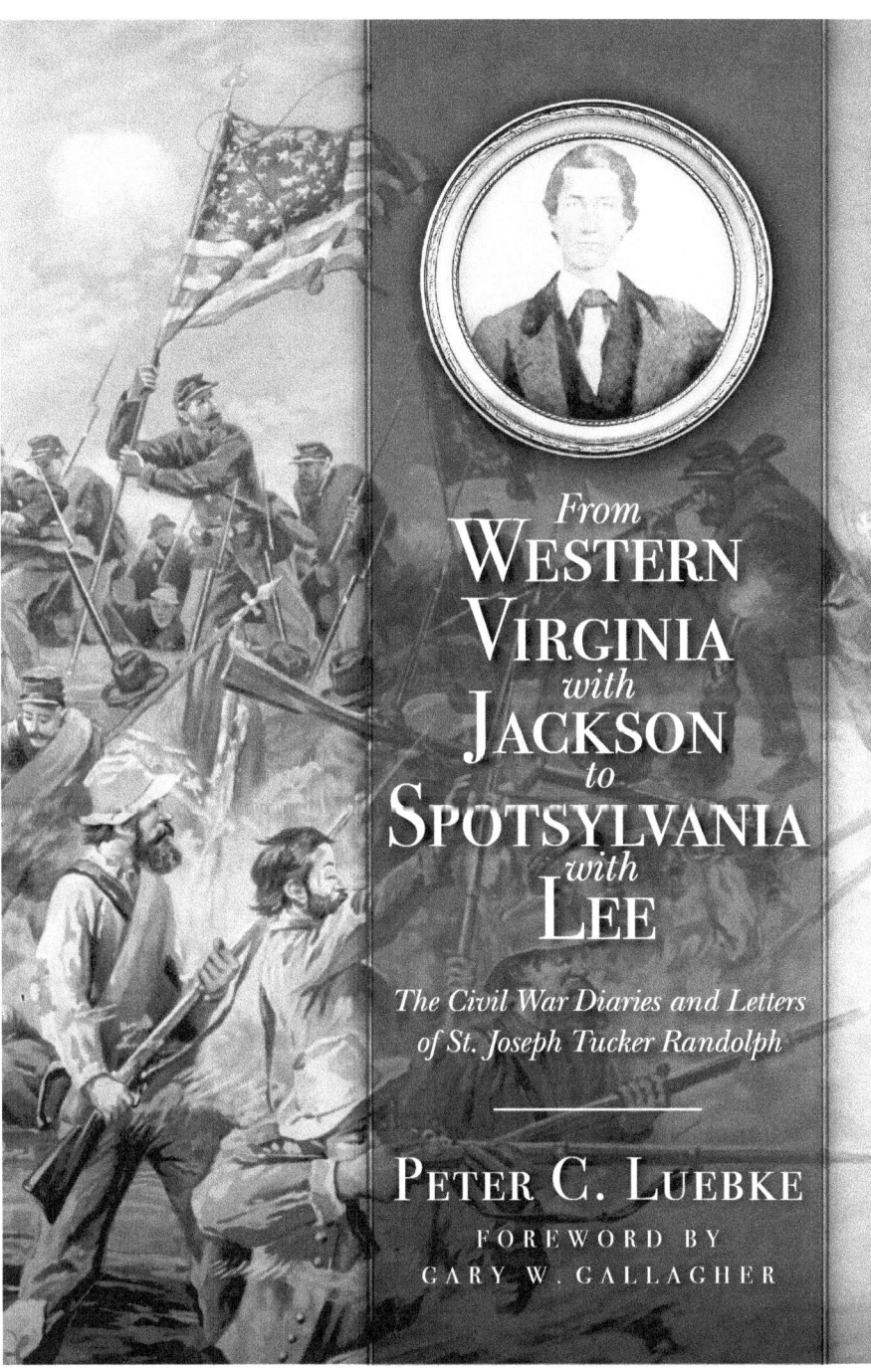

From
WESTERN VIRGINIA
with
JACKSON
to
SPOTSYLVANIA
with
LEE

*The Civil War Diaries and Letters
of St. Joseph Tucker Randolph*

PETER C. LUEBKE

FOREWORD BY
GARY W. GALLAGHER

ISBN-13: 979-8-9865993-8-0
Library of Congress Control Number: 2023933193

35th Star Publishing
Charleston, West Virginia
www.35thstar.com

Cover design by Studio 6 Sense
Interior design by 35th Star Publishing

On the cover:
Painting of the Union Attack on the Bloody Angle at Spotsyvlania Courthouse,
Library of Congress.
Image of St. Joseph Tucker Randolph, courtesy of Mrs. Janet Randolph Turpin Ayers.

Dedicated to John Coski

His scholarship, mentorship, and stewardship of the Eleanor S. Brockenbrough Library have greatly enriched the study of Civil War history.

Table of Contents

Illustrations

Foreword

Americans who lived through the Civil War created a vast body of literary evidence. Reacting to profound disruption in their lives, people in the United States and the Confederacy recorded their thoughts and impressions in correspondence between soldiers at the front and loved ones at home, in diaries and journals kept by women and men, and in reminiscences focused on the war years. More of these firsthand accounts make their way into print every year, swelling the corpus of published primary works available to historians and others interested in the nation's defining crisis. Although few individual witnesses change how we think about the larger contours of the war, their writings provide welcome detail, yield occasional surprises, and remind us anew of the incredibly rich lode of eyewitness testimony from the era.

From Western Virginia with Jackson to Spotsylvania with Lee: The Civil War Diaries and Letters of St. Joseph Tucker Randolph adds a valuable young voice to the swelling chorus from the wartime generation. Ably edited by Peter C. Luebke, who first encountered the documents while under John Coski's tutelage in the Eleanor Brockenbrough Library at the Museum of the Confederacy, Randolph's letters and diaries shed light on various dimensions of the Confederate war effort. For example, readers seeking information about notable military operations will find excellent passages relating to the early stage of the 1862 Valley Campaign, First Kernstown, the Confederate invasion of Kentucky in the autumn of 1862, and the Overland campaign (especially Spotsylvania) - a roster that highlights Randolph's service in both the Eastern and Western Theaters. Twice wounded (the second time mortally), he also saw action in the infantry, the cavalry, and as a staff officer.

Randolph belonged to a notable, though not wealthy, family within Virginia's aristocracy. As a seventeen-year-old in Richmond during the spring of 1861, he observed events closely and readily cast his lot with the Confederacy after his home state seceded. His diary entries convey the excitement, unbridled energy, and swirling rumors of the war's early days. Mustered into the Twenty-First Virginia Infantry in June 1861, he campaigned in the Shenandoah Valley and western Virginia from July through the autumn as part of W. W. Loring's Army of the Northwest. His diary captures the frustrations of hard marches, bad weather, muddy roads, mountain skirmishes, and tedium of life in the ranks during largely unsuccessful operations. Less dramatic than accounts of battles, these entries evoke the reality of day-to-day service that left many men disillusioned and anxious to leave the army.

Growing increasingly disenchanted, Randolph mused about efforts during the winter of 1862-1863 to encourage soldiers to re-enlist and about the threat of a national draft. He imagined joining the artillery after his one-year enlistment ended, or seeking a commission, or even joining the Confederate Marines. Although many of his carping diary entries could be taken as evidence that Randolph cared little about the Confederacy, he maintained a steadfast sense of obligation to the nascent republic. "I think it is a disgrace for anyone like myself who has nothing to keep him out of the field," he wrote in regard to the prospect of being conscripted, "to hold back & be *forced* to fight for his country & this I never intend to do."

Quotable nuggets about prominent military figures enliven the letters and diary entries. On January 19, 1862, for example, Randolph spoke to Thomas J. "Stonewall" Jackson's penchant for secrecy. "[W]e will tramp off to some place," the young infantryman informed his father, "that no one but Old Jack knows anything of, he has the faculty of keeping his plans to himself in a perfect degree, even Genl Loring second in command did not know we were coming here." In Kentucky during the fall of 1862, Randolph lost patience with Braxton Bragg after the Confederate retreat from Perryville. Bragg's promises early in the campaign had buoyed pro-Confederate residents of the crucial Border State, but his withdrawal left them unprotected: "Kentucky is lost to us forever, even were we to drive the Yankees out of the State the people would not believe we were going to stay, and they have good cause for it when one of our *Full Generals* tells them a lie."

Some of Randolph's descriptive passages pull readers into dramatic or poignant scenes. In the fall of 1863, encamped near Rappahannock Station, Virginia, Randolph recounted a recent movement toward Warrenton that revealed the war's harsh effects on a once beautiful and productive area: "[T]he country is completely desolate with some few exceptions, no fences and scarcely a living creature to be seen, the face of the country looks as desolate as you can imagine." A letter to his mother early in 1864 features information about an execution. The victim, "a large man with a very bad face," was "shot for desertion, three times repeated, the day was intensely cold, and the wind blowing 'big guns' we were nearly frozen when we got to camp." Randolph thought his mother "would be surprised to see with what perfect coolness men look on such a sight as this, in half an hour, after, they are just as merry as ever. We were having a game of chess within twenty minutes after those fatal shots were fired."

The voices of Civil War witnesses function much like the dots of color in a Pointillist painting. They complement one another and taken together compose a complex whole. John H. Worsham, whose *One of Jackson's Foot Cavalry* (1912) became a classic, knew Randolph in the Twenty-First Virginia and published an appreciation of his old comrade. Luebke's inclusion of the tribute, penned two days after the anniversary of the battle of First Kernstown in 1901, leaves readers with a sense of how soldiers forged bonds of friendship and loyalty. As Randolph's old regiment maneuvered into position to support an attack near Bethesda Church on the evening of May 30, 1864, Worsham recalled crossing a stream before being ordered to halt. "It was here," he related, "that we heard that Tucker Randolph had been killed in a charge with Pegram's Brigade. Thus died this brilliant soldier boy, just as all soldiers wish to die - at the front, in the thickest of the fight."

Gary W. Gallagher
Charlottesville, Virginia March 3, 2022

Preface

Working with the Tucker Randolph collection was my introduction to the American Civil War. Though a native of Richmond, I had not taken much notice of the Civil War. In college, when I became interested in the history of that conflict, I sought out a way to get into the primary source materials. Thus, I came to the Eleanor Brockenbrough Library at the Museum of the Confederacy as a summer intern. The librarian, John Coski, put me to work immediately, creating finding aids for various collections. An impeccable historian and custodian of the materials in his care, Coski worked to ensure that the Museum of the Confederacy's collections could serve as a resource for scholars.

Exploring that library was a great treat. The connection to the past was always there. One of the collections I created a finding aid for was the Tucker Randolph papers, then part of the MC-3 collection, so named for the Metal Cabinet it had been housed in before the modern era of the museum. Although I did not support the cause for which he fought, I must admit I felt an affinity for Tucker; who was - as we shall see - a bookish young Richmonder caught up in the excitement of the war. It was also exciting for me to handle the diaries and documents. They were the raw materials of history, and with the physical objects in front of me, it was easier to imagine the past.

John Coski encouraged me to transcribe and edit Tucker Randolph's letters and diaries. Impetus was added by the fact that Tucker's grand-niece (the granddaughter of his brother Norman) was alive at the time. Janet Randolph Turpin Ayers (Mrs. David T. Ayers) lived in Richmond and was the family historian. A direct descendent of Tucker's brother Norman, she, too, had been interested in Tucker's papers at the Museum of the Confederacy, but found it difficult to read the photocopies. Early transcripts I made of the letters and diaries allowed her to read the words of her ancestor. I visited with Mrs. Ayers several times and Mrs. Ayers gave me permission to have copies made of the photo of Tucker Randolph and his brother Norman that appears in this book.

This volume represents the culmination of much work. It also represents the beginning of my journey into learning about the Civil War, and I hope that anyone who encounters it will find it enriches their journey.

Acknowledgments

I have been working on this project on and off for nearly two decades, so thank you to everyone who has helped. Many people have read various iterations of the draft and given me good feedback. All of you have helped immensely.

The first people to recognize are my parents, William and Linda Luebke. They have encouraged my learning every step of the way. They also tolerated uncounted boxes of my books in their house through a number of moves. Their support has been instrumental to this endeavor, as well as so many others.

My wife, Veronica Slaght, read and commented on the final drafts of this project. Her background as a newspaper reporter and keen editorial eye definitely sharpened the prose.

Steve Cunningham of 35th Star Publishing has been more patient with me on this project than I had any right to expect, and has done a great job of designing this book.

Numerous Civil War historians have aided this project. Of especial note are the indefatigable Robert K. Krick and Robert E. L. Krick, who both generously provided information from their files, identified leads for me to follow-up on, and otherwise pointed me in the right direction as is their custom. In addition, I have to thank each of them for their respective biographical registers of Confederate colonels and staff officers; my work was made much easier with those references on my desk.

Gary W. Gallagher, my mentor from graduate school, graciously provided a foreword. A titan of Civil War scholarship, what I've learned from Gary has shaped the presentation and annotation of these letters.

I also thank the late Janet Randolph Turpin Ayers for her discussions with me about her family history, as well as the chance to take notes from the family bible. She also allowed me to use the photo of Tucker and Norman Randolph. The late Tucker Hill, a towering figure in the historic preservation community in Richmond, also proved instrumental in securing a copy of the photograph.

Finally, this book is dedicated to John Coski, who gave me my start working in history so many years ago in the Eleanor Brockenbrough Library at the Museum of the Confederacy. John is a model scholar, dedicated to his craft. Moreover, John takes every opportunity to nurture and encourage younger scholars. With the closure of the library at the Museum of the Confederacy and John's retirement, those interested in the Civil War have suffered a real loss. Because of his early suggestion that I edit these letters and his constant support since then, I dedicate this book to John.

Although I have received much aid, all errors, interpretation, and annotation in this book are mine alone.

Introduction

St. Joseph Tucker Randolph belonged to the Randolph family. As some of the first settlers of Virginia, the Randolph family quickly became part of the Tidewater elite. Their earlier generations had been among the most affluent of Virginians. Along with the Lees, Carters, and Tuckers, the Randolphs possessed much economic and political clout during Colonial times.[1] Powerful during the eighteenth century, some branches of the family would fall on hard times.

By the early nineteenth century, however, dissipation had sapped the family fortune. Tucker's father, Joseph Williamson Randolph, was born in Warwick County on August 19, 1815.[2] Joseph Williamson's father, Henry Randolph, suffered from a weakness for horses, among other vices. Family lore held that Henry, a keen rider, "was never known to go through a gate, but always went over it."[3] The recklessness with horse riding also carried over into recklessness in gambling on the horses. One story passed down to Henry's descendants recalled that he took "his wife and daughters to the races in fine carriage drawn by thoroughbred horses, bet both carriage and horses away, and [came] home in a hired hack."[4] Thus, rather than living as scion of a Virginia grandee, Joseph found himself packed off to live with his grandmother at the age of nine due to the behavior of his father.

St. Joseph Tucker Randolph (left)
and his younger brother Norman Vincent Randolph (right)
Courtesy of Mrs. Janet Randolph Turpin Ayers

Joseph Williamson made his way to the state capital of Richmond in 1829, starting a career as a stationer and bookseller at the age of fourteen. He began work at the store of John H. Nash at a starting salary of fifty dollars a year. When Nash's store went out of business in 1831, Joseph purchased the remaining stock and opened his own store in on 12th Street in Richmond. This store failed, too, and Joseph moved to Norfolk to work in his uncle Josiah Abbott's store in 1834. He remained there until 1842, when the store relocated to Richmond[5]

In Norfolk, Joseph met his future wife, Honoria Mary Tucker. Born in Alexandria on December 1, 1816, into another family with a long Virginia pedigree, Nora lived in Norfolk with her brother, John "Handsome Jack" Randolph Tucker of the United States Navy. Nora and Joseph married on November 26, 1842 in Norfolk, after which Nora relocated to Richmond to live with Joseph.[6] The couple's first child, St. Joseph Tucker Randolph, arrived on September 19, 1843. Three years later followed their second child, Norman Vincent Randolph, on November 2, 1846.[7]

Little is known of Tucker's childhood, though he likely attended private schools in Richmond, as did his brother. Tucker and Norman were raised in the Catholic faith (Nora was Catholic and Joseph converted to the faith). Both brothers were baptized at St. Peter's Catholic Church in Richmond and both brothers evinced a deep belief in their faith. Tucker wrote to Bishop John McGill, the preacher at St. Peter's, during the Civil War about how to reconcile Lenten practices with duty in the field while others commented that Norman was "very devout" and that his "religion was too real--not obtrusive, not sentimental-it seemed just to be the principle of life with him."[8]

In 1849, Josiah Abbot died and Joseph Williamson Randolph took over the bookstore. Joseph grew the business into a successful concern and claimed his bookstore and bindery was "equal in quality and finish to any other house in the Southern States." Modern historians have confirmed that opinion, noting that "Randolph was, if not the most prominent, certainly one of the most active of his calling in Richmond." Joseph's publishing endeavors suggest a Southern nationalism; his store published books by noted Southern nationalist Edmund Ruffin and the first successful law journal in the South. Tucker, when old enough, helped clerk in the store. From his father he likely inherited loyalty to the South.[9]

While the Randolph family ran a bookstore and could be classed as merchants, they also owned enslaved people. Joseph paid taxes on four enslaved people in 1859 and 1860, though by the 1860 census, the family owned three. He likely had them work a small farm he owned or hired them out. Holding that many slaves was not unusual for white Virginians. Thus, while Tucker himself held no human property, his family did and benefitted from the institution. It can be inferred that between Southern nationalist printing and slave ownership, the Randolph family would have found justification for supporting secession among increasing sectional tensions.[10]

As war tensions between the North and South increased, Tucker joined a local elite volunteer militia company in 1860, when he was still seventeen. This unit, F Company, resembled more of a social and recreational club than a professional fighting outfit. Many of its members came from the upper ranks of society. The men wore elaborate uniforms of cadet gray with gilt buttons and extensive gold braiding on the cuffs. Members wore white gloves while on duty. The men also sported hairy calfskin knapsacks, specially imported from Paris. One member of F Company recalled that these unusual bags "were divided into partitions" with "openings into some of these partitions so that one could handles articles inside without opening the whole knapsack." Although F Company functioned as a social outlet, its members did receive training in drill and other military matters. Its members would serve as nucleus for Confederate forces once the Civil War began. Of the 192 members of F Company at the start of the Civil War, 57 men would become officers in the Confederate Army.[11]

Thus, as war loomed after the election of Abraham Lincoln in November 1860 and the secession of South Carolina in December, followed by other Deep South states in early 1861, Tucker found himself in the capital of Virginia and a member of a unit sure to see action if fighting broke out.

Editorial Method

This volume presents Tucker's diaries and letters as he wrote them. The collection contained a small pocket diary, a larger diary, and numerous letters. This edition presents the full text of all of those, as well as the full text of two recollections by Tucker's wartime comrades. Spelling and grammar has not been corrected. Only cosmetic changes have been made, such as standardizing the date line for diary entries and letters and lowering superscripts to the line.

Anything that appears in italics within squared brackets [like this] has been added by the editor for the purposes of clarity. Text that Tucker scratched through but was still legible has been included, but struck through ~~like this~~.

I've limited my explanations of the people, places, and events that Tucker describes to the endnotes. When reading primary sources, such as these, I prefer an experience uninterrupted by editorial intervention.

6   From Western Virginia with Jackson to Spotsylvania with Lee

1
Rumors of Wars
April 9 to April 30, 1861

In Spring 1861, a sense of uncertainty and excitement gripped Richmond, the capital of Virginia. Over the winter, the states of the Deep South had seceded and formed the Confederate States of America. Confederate President Jefferson Davis had called for militia, and the nascent Confederate States Army invested Fort Sumter in Charleston Harbor, as well as several other Federal fortifications. Federal authorities had sent resupply by sea, but both sides still cautiously eyed the other. While the Deep South moved energetically, the states of the Upper South still debated about whether or not to leave the Union. In Virginia, a convention had been sitting since February, and despite the inauguration of Abraham Lincoln, its members counseled caution and Union. Virginians tried to broker compromise between the Deep South and the Federal government, with a commission leaving for Washington in early April. The Unionist delegates still prevailed in April 1861, with the Virginia Convention voted against secession. Virginia had not yet been forced to take a side.

Tucker Randolph began his diary entries at this moment, recording his thoughts at the end of the day. Like many other young white Virginians, Tucker supported secession.[1] He had also joined F Company, a Richmond militia unit in preparation for war. While he drilled with the unit, he still continued to help his father at the family bookstore. Tucker's writings give an eyewitness look at the early heady days of Virginia's secession.

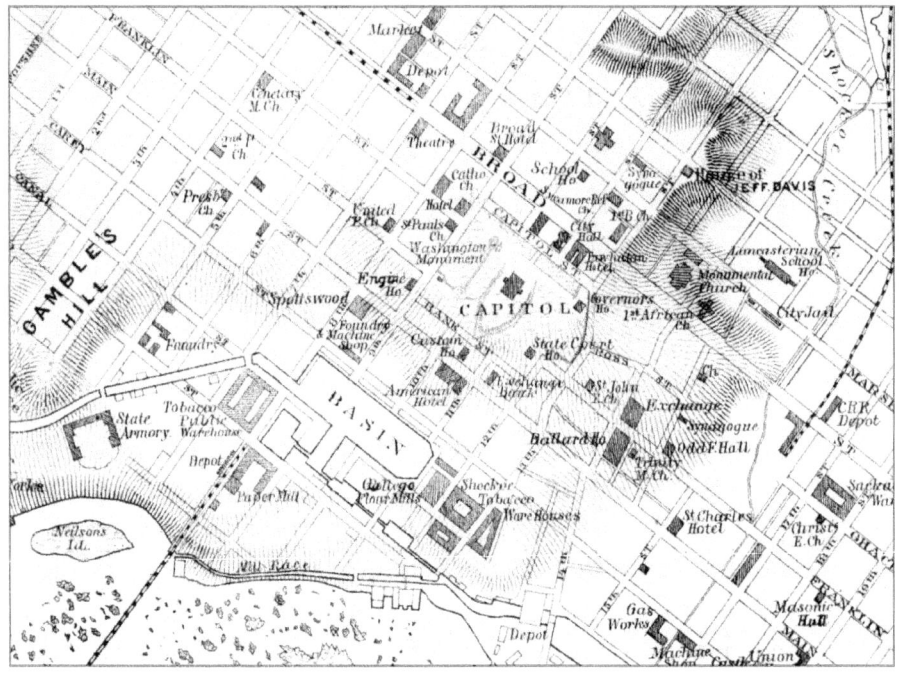

Richmond City during the Civil War.
A detail of a map of central Richmond during the Civil War. In the center of the map is the Virginia Capitol and Capitol Square. To the west of Capitol Square is the Spotswood Hotel on Main Street where Tucker and F Company met. Further west along Main Street lay J. W. Randolph's Bookstore at 121 Main Street. The Richmond City Poor House (officially known as the Alms House) lay to the north of Capitol Square, off of this map. Rockett's Landing lay to the south east, also off this map.
Library of Congress Prints and Photographs Division
http://hdl.loc.gov/loc.gmd/g3884r.cw0645700

Tuesday, April 9th, 1861, Diary Entry

I have just come from drill, in consequence of the rain (which has continued since Saturday with a few intermissions) we had a very small number present.

Pa has not been in since Saturday, I suppose on account of the bad weather.

The rumors afloat are pregnant with War. the dispatches say that a Fleet of seven or more vessels are lying of[f] the harbor of Charleston, with the intention if possible of reinforcing the Fort.[2]

The Political atmosphere is dark in the extreme.

Commissioners viz Messrs Preston Stuart & Randolph have been sent to Washington to inquire the policy of the Government.[3]

Secession is steadily gaining ground in the Convention.

Mr Peyton Johnston's youngest child died yesterday. Business is very much depressed. Change is very scarce.

Broke the Chrystal of my watch at drill.

Wednesday, April 10th, 1861, Diary Entry

It has rained all day but seems to be clearing off now (10 o'clock).

The river[4] is very high & rising rapidly

No Political news of any moment, except the Commander of the Squadron outside the harbor Charleston says he will reinforce the fort peaceably if he can but forcibly if he must

Received a letter from Peyton

Friday, April 12th, 1861, Diary Entry

I went out home yesterday evening so did not get a chance to write.

Went to the river yesterday, it is very high the water has been in Main St but today it has subsided very much.

It is raining now very hard it commenced this evening early.

We had a little dance in the Parlor tonight. Miss Mary May from Petersburg is here.

I went to an evening entertainment at Col Dimmock's[5] and have just come home. it is now 1 1/2 o'clock. So I must to bed.

Fort Sumpter, so the telegrams say has been bombarded. Commenced at 4 1/2 this morning.[6] There was a collision between Daniel & Johnson,[7] but no damage done.

Saturday, April 13th, 1861, Diary Entry

This has been an eventful day, one long to be remembered.

There was great excitement here all day, in consequence of Telegrams, which reported first that Fort Sumpter had surrendered & again that there was a white flag on the ramparts.[8]

Salutes were fired at the Armory & on the square, the Fayette[9] turned out their guns <u>without</u> the Governor's[10] permission & fired a hundred salutes, I think. Then a Secession Flag was carried to the Governor's house to get permission to hoist it on the Capitol, but he refused & made a speech which I did not hear, the flag was brought in the Capitol & carried by Main force to the Standard on top & Hoisted amid the Cheers of a large concourse of People. There was quite a crowd in the Capitol that when we ran up stairs, there was a general rush. The roof was crowded, myself among the No. The Governor has since had it taken down & a guard posted around the C. We had a great many speeches, the best from Mssrs Patton, Gordon, Sheffey & others whose names I don't know.[11]

After Supper there was a grand procession through the City, with Music, Confederacy Flags, Transparencies, Torches, &c, also Bonfires or Tar Barrels, Boxes &c amid shots [of] rockets & Roman Candles. I hear music now as I write this (11 1/2).

Monday, April 15th, 1861, Diary Entry

I went out home yesterday, it was a very delightful day. I also took a ride & went to see the McRae's. Dr Friend is very sick, he is threatened with consumption.

Went out to the Poor house with about 20 Men Co F, the Ordnance Dep. Capt Elliott[12] & others to try McEvoy's Cartridge the performance is decidedly in favor of it.[13]

Great excitement all day. Lincoln has made a demand for 3000 Men.[14] It is reported an Ordnance of Secession will be passed to-morrow. Stuart, Baldwin & others have turned.[15]

Went to see Miss Tyler. Saw Misses Russell & Vale. Miss Lizzie was not in the Misses R & V are very pleasant Ladies both Unionists & both from <u>Mass</u> I believe. Went to Selden's Room for the first time. Charlie & Mr. Royster have become Secessionists.[16] Botts[17] is a Revolutionist & it is said Scott & Lee have resigned.[18]

The Virginia Capitol Building in 1865.
During April 1861, the Capitol hosted the Secession Convention.
Record Group 111, Matthew Brady Photographs of Civil War-Era Personalities and Scenes, National Archives. Identifier 529087

Tuesday, April 16th, 1861, Diary Entry

It has been raining again to-day & is raining now.

A good deal of excitement all day.

It is rumored that there is a Revenue Cutter in the River.

The York River Road has been somewhat damaged by recent rains.

We had a meeting on the Square but in consequence of the rain, did nothing but make arrangements to elect some new members.

The Convention has been sitting with closed doors all day & this evening, no one knows what they have done, but it is supposed an Ordnance of Secession has been passed.[19]

There are Wars & Rumors of Wars[20] quite plentiful today, but nothing definite.

Thursday, April 18th, 1861, Diary Entry

I did not write last night because I did not come home.

Yesterday about 3 o'clock there was a great excitement down town, we were ordered out to assemble at Rockets,[21] but did not know what we were to do. I ran up & put on my accoutrements & ran down to Rockets. When I got there I found that the *Yorktown* had been seized & 7 others stayed on board all night to guard her & were relieved this morning. the *Jamestown* has since been seized also.[22]

Could not get a Colt's Pistol in town but got a Beals Patent.[23]

We rendezvoused under the Spotswood[24] had about 30 odd new recruits & received names of a good many more. We were ordered down in Knapsacks, all packed, & a signal of 6 bells to assemble to-night in case of need.

Great political excitement.

Gen Scott has resigned & been arrest by Lincoln for Treason, so reported.[25] Carlile reported to have been arrested in Alexandria for divulging the secret proceedings of the Convention to Lincoln.[26]

Uncle John with several other officers has resigned to-day.[27]

The Spotswood Hotel, seen from Main Street in 1865.
Tucker and Company F met here in 1861.
Library of Congress Prints and Photographs Division,
https://hdl.loc.gov/loc.pnp/cwpb.00458

Tucker's uncle, Captain John Randolph Tucker served in the Confederate States Navy.

Quinby & Co, photographer. Captain John Randolph Tucker of the Confederate States Navy and Confederate States Prov Navy in uniform / Quinby & Co., photographic artists, Charleston, S.C. Library of Congress Prints and Photographs Division, https://www.loc.gov/item/2022630164/

Friday, April 19th, 1861, Diary Entry

We received telegram from Baltimore to-day stating that the 7th Regiment of Mass. had been attacked by the people as it attempted to pass through to Washington & had quite a sharp engagement in which a good many had been Killed on both sides, but it was reported that the Regiment had been almost cut to pieces, there was great rejoicing here at the news & shout after shout was given with a will.[28]

A Naval Officer who it was reported had dispatches for Lincoln from Portsmouth was arrested this evening at the Petersburg depot, he is a fine looking fellow & named Walters. he had some ladies with him who were very much frightened.

bought a Colts five shooter to-day gave twenty dollars for it.

We had a great torch light procession this evening, the houses all over the city were light up, rockets were fired &c we have been drilling every night at 8 o'clock & have drills all day for new members under the Spottswood.

Graniss bade us all good bye to-day, he is going home to New York.[29]

Saturday, April 20th, 1861, Diary Entry

I have been restless all day, waiting for orders, have been in undress uniform all day. The Norfolk people have taken, it is reported, the Navy Yard, with a large quantity of Munitions of War.[30]

There are some of the Norfolk troops here come up this morning

We were ordered to assemble at our quarters under the Spottswood this evening at 8 o'c, in full uniform with Knapsack packed.

We were mustered in ranks all prepared for March when the order was countermanded & we wait with savage hearts were dismissed with orders to assemble to-morrow (Sunday) at the Barracks, in full uniform for dress drill at 8 1/2 o'c. The companies are fast filling up. The Regt will be divided into two & it is likely F. Co will be also.

1861

He carried a knapsack, containing a jacket, white vest, dress shirts, collars, white gloves, toothbrush, undershirts, drawers, socks, soap, towels, needlecase, with needles, thread and buttons; an oilcloth, blanket, extra shoes, canteen, haversack, and tin cup.

A depiction of an F Company soldier in 1861, when their equipment was new and reflected the spit and polish of an antebellum social group more than a fighting unit.

Worsham, *One of Jackson's Foot Cavalry*

Sunday, April 21st, 1861, Diary Entry

We were ordered out at 8 o'c for Regimental drill. We went out to an old field near Hollywood & drilled for some time, when we marched back to town & as we were on the Square & about to march back to Barracks the Signal of 6 taps of the bell sounded & we received orders to prepare for a march. there was intense excitement, everywhere, particularly in the Churches, Ladies fainted & young men running out. I had a visit from Ma & a whole platoon of others which came near upsetting my applecart but after some delay we started for Rockets, & as we supposed to go on a Steamer down the River as the object of the expedition was to prevent the *Pawnee* a U.S. vessel[31] from coming up the river but when we arrived at Rockets, we met the Col Moore[32] & some of his staff coming back, then we received orders to march down to Wilton[33] on the river about 10 miles where the Howitzers[34] had marched before us we passed the Fayette[35] at Powhatan, they came on after us, we had quite a rough road to travel, but we arrived at Wilton in the evening & planted the Artillery on the Bank. After dark our Knapsacks arrived & we had supper, which consisted of half done Bacon & Bread, & crackers, but it was devoured with great relish we spread out on the grass by the Guns, those that had blankets the new recruits were not very well equipped. Col Knight[36] very kindly allowed them to sleep in the parlors & gave a good many meals. Miss Lieu Watkins[37] came over, she said to nurse the wounded, but we had no need of her services. During the night one of the sentinels fired at a schooner. We all sprang up but allowed her to pass. We had Breakfast in the morning ([*April*] 22) same as supper. About mid-day we were ordered back, a Lighter & Tug came down for us, we formed in line the Artillery men in front & F in the rear. The Fayette marched in the hold, the Howitzers & F on deck but when all were aboard, the Artillery men refused to stay in the hold, so Capt. Cary (Senior Captain)[38] marched the F boys down, & the grumbles came on deck, which made them feel quite sheepish. We sang & danced nearly all the way up. When we landed, we marched up Main to Barracks & dismissed with orders to hold ourselves in readiness for orders. We were in uniforms all day Tuesday [*April 23*], but received no orders and had a drill at 8 o'c at the Barracks.

Captain R. Milton Cary led F Company at the
time of its entry into Confederate service.
Worsham, *One of Jackson's Foot Cavalry*

Rockett's Landing lay southeast of Richmond on the James River.
Library of Congress Prints and Photographs Division,
https://loc.gov/pictures/resource/stereo.1s04641/

I was awakened about 2 1/2 o'c on Wednesday [*April 24*] morning by Charley Crane[39] & told to assemble at Barracks at once, where our Arms & Accoutrements had been in readiness for some time. I jumped in Clothes & boots, threw my coat on my arm & put out for the Barracks double quick. When I got there, was sent out to hunt up the men, most of them arrived in time we left on the cars about 7 o'c, with 95 men for Fredericksburg, took breakfast at Ashland & came on to F[redericksburg]. On arrival we were quartered in the Court House & literally carried by storm, by the hospitable people of the Town, to their houses. Our quarters were crowded by gentlemen at meal times, the Blues[40] were with us.

Thursday, April 25th, 1861, Diary Entry

Capt Cary had the stalls of the Fair Ground near town fitted up for us, with straw & cotton tacked on the face of each stall, in the shape of curtains, some 3 or 4 with myself slept there that night to guard the place, each on guard 2 hours. We drew straws. I had the 1st guard, the best.

Friday, April 26th, 1861, Diary Entry

We marched out to camp with the Bs[41] & took possession, 3 in a Stall, Bob White John Cowardin[42] & Myself in one, here was formed the *Pawnee* Mess.

Our routine is as follows, with little variation Reveille at 5 o'c & roll call, drill, then we started about Breakfast, which consists of Bacon & Bakers Bread, Coffee, which we make better than I expected, & anything else we can get, Eggs, Fish &c After Breakfast, wash up everything, & take a smoke, then drill for the recruits & instructors detailed for the new companies, of which there are some 6 or 7, dinner, at 2 o'c, same as breakfast, after dinner a dress drill, & Parade at 5 o'c, when we are dismissed & a great many go to talk to the Girls of which there is a goodly number, others prepare supper same as Breakfast, then we chat until around 10 o'c, when Tattoo beats, & roll call at 10 1/2 Tapps, when all lights must be out & every thing quiet, or clap them in the Guard House.

Sunday, April 28th, 1861, Diary Entry

It rained to-day but most of the men went to town, it is quite cool.

We had a dress drill & Parade & Review by Genl Ruggles[43] of the Old Army.

A man named Crump was dismissed from Walkers Battery[44] for insubordination.

Monday, April 29th, 1861, Diary Entry

It was quite cool last night & blowing hard as it was all day yesterday. Several of our men came up from Richmond with letters, packages &c.

2
Expecting an Attack
May 1 to July 18, 1861

After the excitement of the *Pawnee* Affair, Tucker and his comrades settled into a routine around Fredericksburg. Periodic scares of invasion livened the days, as Virginians waited for the inevitable advance of Union forces. By the end of June, F Company mustered into Confederate service, becoming part of the 21st Virginia Infantry Regiment.

Wednesday, May 1st, 1861, Diary Entry

I am detailed for Guard to-day. It is blowing very hard & cold.

Thursday, May 22nd, 1861, Diary Entry

Had a very cold time on Guard last night. I was cold with my overcoat on I thought my guard from 2 to 4 the longest two hours I ever passed we are on post 2 & off 4 hours. The place is full of the most extravigant rumors.

I sent in an application for furlough, but do not know the time, for days. I went home & while I was gone, the company left for Aquia Creek.

I went up immediately, slept at an old camp that night & arrived at Aquia Creek, in an hour so. We were quartered in a house on a hill called Game Point we could see the River very well. The Blues were near Walkers Battery,[1] & Shore Battery at the Landing, of 8in Columbiads 2 in number.[2] Capt Cary was appointed Lt. Col. while we were in Fredericksburg. Capt Lynch, Lieut Simms of the Navy were at the Point.[3]

Friday, May 24th, 1861, Diary Entry

We were rather startled yesterday at seeing 3 or 4 steamers off the Point, rather near this side, but on a tree being cut down which nearly masked the Battery, the vessels steamed off. We were ordered to pack up, which we did in a short time, but there was no need of us A squad was drilling on the warf one of the Steamers thinking to run them off, ran out some of her guns, but the men stood their ground. Man Page[4] was drilling them, the River is about 5 miles wide here.

We send out a Picket every night across the creek as a lookout, a beacon is ready on the beach to give the alarm, the Post is on the Potomac bank, at a Scrim windlass.

Vessels pass continuously up the River carrying troops &c. The Boat *George Page* is safe in the Creek.[5] We were out on a Scout yesterday

Mann Page of F Company stood his ground when surprised by a Union warship near Fredericksburg

Chamberlayne, *Ham Chamberlayne, Virginian*

evening for 2 fellows who had been larking about, but we saw nothing of them.

Thursday, May 30th 1861, Diary Entry

There are 4 of us here (Potomac Creek Bridge) to guard it, there is a Battery on the opposite side of 2 Columbiads commanded by Lieut Alexander of Fred.[6]

We heard firing from the Creek yesterday. We fired a signal to bring up troops from Fred. there was a good deal of excitement, the troops did not come up until night, but there was no need of them. We were on duty the whole of last night. I stood on one post half the night. We are about 8 miles from the creek.

2 Steamers came up to the Battery & gave them a round which was answered, & some 15 or 20 rounds were exchanged pretty brisk, no damage done to our side, but it is thought we struck the vessels several times, they soon moved off.[7] F & the Blues were on the edge of the marsh to repel any attempt to land.

Letter, Thursday, May 30th 1861

Potomac Creek Bridge Battery

Dear Pa,

Thinking there may be a great many rumors about a little affair yesterday, I drop you a few lines to let you know I am safe. There is four of us here at the Bridge to guard it.

On yesterday we heard the report of heavy guns in quick succession from the creek & answered them from our Battery here as a signal to bring up troops from Fredericksburg, there was a great deal of excitement here at the firing & troops came up last night from <u>Fred</u>, but after the fight was over. We were up all last night on duty expecting an attack but nothing happened. We heard the news of the fight this morning (we are about 8 miles from the creek). Two steamers came opposite the Battery, only 2 guns & fired at it. We answered it & some 15 or more rounds each was fired hot & heavy. Co F & the Blues were on the edge of the marsh to repel any attempt to land, which they did not attempt. No one was hurt except a slight scratch on the head of one of the men but the Capt is sure that we struck her some 3 or 4 times & one shell burst on her deck, after which she put up the River & have not seen her since.

We expect to go to Manassas Gap, to rejoin the 1st Regt.[8]

All well, love to all, did you get my letter & have you gotten the Comm-.[9]

Your Affectionate Son,

Tucker

P.S. Since writing the above I received yours [of the] 29th. I supposed there was a great many applications for commissions but several of F. Co have received them who are very poor soldiers so I think there is some chance yet "don't give up the ship."

Friday, May 31st, 1861, Diary Entry

We came up from the Bridge to Camp Game Point. The vessels made another demonstration we packed up & marched down to near an old Wood Shed, the shells flew all around us but not harm was done, except some of the shells tore the rails on the road. A train of cars was going to the Point but put back, a shell came very near striking them. We went back to camp.

Saturday, June 1st, 1861, Diary Entry

The Yanks came to their work again to-day. The *Pawnee* & several Gun Boats, & 1 or 2 steamers commenced hot & heavy. We packed up hastily & went quick time down & passed behind a hill to protect us from their fire, the Bs were with us, a good many of us crept to the top & saw the affair very well some 600 shot & shell were thrown by the enemy. We did not throw so often, they shot at our camp but did no harm, & threw some over our heads, only one man was hurt on our side, slightly on the head, the enemies loss was quite heavy. Capt Ward of the *Pawnee* was killed & the vessel damaged. We returned to camp about dark.[10]

An engagement from later in June 1861. *Thomas Freeborn* (on the left) and *Pawnee*
(on the right) engage the Confederate land batteries at Aquia Creek.
Drawn by Alfred R. Waud. Library of Congress Prints and Photographs Division,
https://lccn.loc.gov/2004660792

Friday, June 7th, 1861, Diary Entry

We were aroused by a gun from the Point, & the news that 3 or 4,000
Yanks had landed above us & were coming down on us we packed up &
crossed the creek in boats after marching a short distance. We met the
blues & Walkers Battery coming back, they were stationed on that side,
the origin of the report, was, a boat which was fired on containing 2 men
who escaped, but the boat was taken so we had to return from another
"*Pawnee*" Affair.

After dark, Lieut Welford[11] with 50 men, myself among them started
for a place [on] the River about 4 miles down where the Yanks were
supposed to be attempting to land it rained hard & quite cool the mud
was awful & dark as Erebus[12] we took our position by an old fish house
& kept sentinels on the beach. We could see the lights of the vessels very
plainly but the night passed off very disagreeably but no Yanks came, so
we left for Camp in the morning tired & used up.

About this time I made Corporal & Capt. Cunningham elected.[13] We frequently had scouts to look for suspicious characters generally at night.

I was with Dick Robinson[14] one night & returning I heard some noise in the bushes, when a hog jumped out with a loud snort & Dick's Pistol went off, the ball passing me quite close.

There were 2 10in Columbiads sent up, to be mounted, they weigh over 9000pds. All the oxen they could get could not get them up, so getting to-gether all the men they could we hitched on & drew them up after great difficulty on a high hill. the second one broke the Carry-All, but got another. We worked till after mid-night. they were Pivot guns.

Thursday, June 13th, 1861, Diary Entry

We arrived in Richmond, orders had been sent for us some time, but were detained by Col Cary, some of our boys were sent to the Tennessee & Arkansas Regts to drill them, but all got together again[15] Capt Wise tried to get the Company to go with him in the Wise Legion,[16] but we declined when we passed through Fredericksburg there were a great many of the town folks to see us. Lange who had made us visits at Game Point, with his Cake, Ice Cream &c, gave us a very nice refreshment at the depot Lemon-Aide &c. the blues were with us.

We arrived at Richmond on the evening & marched to our old Barracks, right glad to be home again. We kept a guard there day & night over our Muskets &c.

Troops are continually arriving.

Friday, June 28th, 1861, Diary Entry

We were mustered into service to-day at 10 o'c by Genl Baldwin,[17] & marched back to Barracks. We had a dress drill on the Square one evening at which there was a great crowd of young ladies &c, all pronounced it No 1, some the best they had ever saw our platoon was so long that the files had to broken off to get by the "Skirts."

Saturday, June 29th, 1861, Diary Entry

We bade good bye to our old barracks at 9 o'c & marched out to the New Fair Grounds Camp Lee, where we found Co B from Baltimore who gave us 3 cheers & we saluted them.

Our wagons came up, but the ground was wet, so we went to work cleared it off but did not pitch our tents til evening, got supper & tumbled in 8 in our tent, quite a close fit, but we slept like bricks.

Sunday, June 30th, 1861, Diary Entry

We prepared for Inspection but it rained so we did not have it. A certain No are allowed to go to town each day but require passes, others run the Blockade. Our tents leak at first.

Monday, July 1st, 1861, Diary Entry

It rained a good deal to-day, in the evening we had our 1st Parade, here with Co B who are next to us, & the Madison Infantry from Louisiana,[18] after Parade we were marched with Co B to the Penitentiary, through the rain & mud, which was on fire.[19] We soon arrived. All the workshops were well burnt we were marched to town after the fire was nearly out & dismissed til next morning at 10 o'c. I staid with John Pizzini.

Tuesday, July 2nd, 1861, Diary Entry

We [assembled] according to order at 10 o'c & marched to camp.

Nothing of any note took place, for the next few weeks we were at Camp Lee except we went to Gilhams Regiment, also Co B.[20] We had Squad & company drill & Parades at which a good many Ladies & Gentlemen came out. We frequently had some of them to supper with us, the weather was very warm.

Thursday, July 18th, 1861, Diary Entry

We received [orders] last night to strike our tents & be ready to move early in the morning. We were aroused quite early & set to work to strike tent & pack up, but Col Gilham had to come & hurry us up. We finally got off & marched off down to the Central Depot, it was very hot & some came near fainting, after waiting some time we were put in Box Cars, with benches. Pa, Norman & Harlin were there & a crowd of the friends & relations of the boys, & rather a Lachrimose affair, after a great deal of delay we left finally at 10 o'c but stopd very often, reached Gordonsville about 6 o'c we heard that Genl Garnett was certainly dead & Col Pegram a prisoner.[21]

A later view of John Pizzini, one of Tucker's friends from F Company.
Author's collection

Western Virginia

0   Miles   30
Map by Edward Alexander

PENNSYLVANIA

Hancock

Cumberland

Bath

MARYLAND

Martinsburg

Potomac River

Grafton

Romney

Clarksburg

Winchester

Philippi

Kernstown

Strasburg

Shenandoah River

Woodstock

WEST VIRGINIA

Mount Jackson

Valley Mountain

Culpeper C.H.

Monterey

Harrisonburg

McDowell

Elk Mountain

Jennings Gap

Orange C.H.

Edray

Greenbrier River

Buffalo Gap

Gordonsville

Huntersville

Staunton

VIRGINIA

Charlottesville

Clifton Forge

Lewisburg

James River

North

Greenbrier Bridge

Lexington

3
To the Valley and Western Virginia
July 19 to December 1861

In the summer of 1861, several Northern advances threatened the Confederate position in Virginia. Union forces menaced northwestern Virginia, a region particularly vulnerable after a stinging defeat at Rich Mountain. Reinforcements headed west to shore up the Confederate line. F Company was one of the units dispatched.

As Tucker's diaries and letters make clear, the new soldiers had to march across rough terrain. Not yet seasoned to the harsh realities of military campaigning, the men of F Company would soon be broken in to life in the army. The troops rode the train west to Staunton, and after that they marched west, across the Allegheny Mountains and to the Greenbrier River. Tucker's command operated in that general area until November, when they march back to Staunton, Virginia. By December, they had shifted north to Winchester.

Friday, July 19th, 1861, Diary Entry

We arrived here (Staunton) about 8 o'c we had a very uncomfortable night, slept in the cars, which were very crowded, it was quite cold at night, the mountains are beautiful I rode part of the way on top of the cars had a fine view

~~July 20th~~ heard of Beauregard's ~~& Johnson's~~ victory at Bull Run.[1] We slept on a hill above the American Hotel It rained during the night, so we had to pitch our tents, ~~we move in the morning~~ We hired a waggon to carry our knapsacks to H.

Sunday, July 21st, 1861, Diary Entry

Left Staunton about 9 o'c yesterday passing through the town to the Monterey road, after a rough march of 10 miles we reached Buffalo Gap, we left the Battalion behind us, we arrived about 2 o'c & pitched our tents, the scenery along the road is very fine, we leave in the morning for another march of 15 or 20 miles, our boys stood the march very well.

~~July 22nd.~~ We left this morning about 8 o'c & reached Jennings Gap about 1 o'c the road is very rough & several mountains had to be crossed but we made it very well. We had to leave some of [our] Mess Chests at Buffalo Gap, 5 to the Company so the messes had to couple, we heard Guns distinctly from Manassas, about the time we halted, we went to the creek & had a wash, our feet were quite sore.[2]

Monday, July 22nd, 1861, Diary Entry

We struck our tents, packed up, & left Jenning's Gap about 7 o'c, soon after we started it set in to rain, the road was very rough & numerous mountains, the mud was very disagreeable, we arrived at McDowell's tired, wet, muddy, cold & foot sore, the rain came down very hard, we were completely drenched, our tents not having arrived yet, we collected around the fires of some men who we found encamped here, trying to warm & dry, our waggons came at last, we pitched tents in the rain & cooked something the best we could the distance was between 16 or 17 miles.

Tuesday, July 23rd, 1861, Diary Entry

Left camp at 8 o'c & had a very rough march the country is very mountainous, it rained part of the day, we arrived at Monterey at 12 o'c, having march 10 miles, our feet were very sore, many had blisters, but we bathed them in the branches, which gives great relief, we found some few troops here & an Artillery Co. Col Scott & Regt, the people are very bitter against him,[3] the scenery is magnificent, we have orders to prepare for a march of 26 miles to-morrow, a great many reports are flying about, Genl McClellan is advancing to Staunton, said to be 8 or 10,000 men about here, McC is said to have 40,000 Genl Jackson in command.[4]

Wednesday, July 24th, 1861, Diary Entry

Were roused about 4 o'c & struck tents too, & passed through Monterey a very small place at 8 1/2, struck a very rough road, over which we marched 14 miles camping about 3 o'c in a very pretty valley the roads are terrible on the feet, being very rocky our waggons arrived quite late.

Thursday, July 25th, 1861, Diary Entry

Reveille beat about 3 o'c we left about 7 o'c & reached Napp's Creek 1 o'c coming 12 miles, had only 52 men in line out of nearly a hundred. The enemy are said to be in 14 miles of Huntersville, but we do not credit it.

Friday, July 26th, 1861, Diary Entry

Left Napp's Creek at 7 o'c 7 arrived at the miserable looking town of Huntersville, about 12 o'c, 8 miles, the worse road we have passed over, so far, numerous branches to cross, the Regulars & Col Burke's[5] Regt 42nd are with us. Col Gilham in command,[6] a great many rumors are floating about it is very warm some of the boys killed a large Rattlesnake.

Tuesday, July 30th, 1861, Diary Entry

Col Patton[7] joined us here, a good many men are unwell from the Limestone water. I have just gotten off guard. It is warm in the day, but it is quite cold at night making an overcoat very comfortable. I slept on the ground by the fire, when off duty the tent was full & one was filled with prisoners, unionists. The dews are very heavy coming through the tent. We are waiting for some Provisions from Milboro Depot, our waggons left some several days ago, it is 35 miles, we expect when they come to move forward we have had no sugar for some time we paid for hauling our knapsacks 1.33 each.

Genl Loring[8] takes command of this division called "Army of the Northwest."

We have some very good looking Cavalry & 1 artillery Co. Col Gilham has been on a Scout towards Valley Mountain.

Thursday, August 1st, 1861, Diary Entry

I am Picket duty to-day,[9] nothing of any note is happening that we can hear of. It rained all morning very hard, we are very tired of Camp Col Burke's 42nd left about 1 o'c & a piece of artillery from Marye's Battery. We had a hunt for a Rattlesnake in the night, could hear him rattle but could not see him.

Saturday, August 3rd, 1861, Diary Entry

The left wing left yesterday, we struck our tents & were ready to leave when a violent storm came up & we were completely wet Knapsacks & all. We left however at 6 1/2 P.M. with our Knapsacks on our backs, wet & cold, the road got worse as we advanced, we reached camp where the Left Wing was, about 12 o'c, wet & completely exhausted. I suffered perfect agony all the way, it was dark, one of our boys D. B. Jones[10] came very [near] being killed by rolling off the road, the men would throw themselves on the road side completely used up, we laid down by the fires left burning, on the wet ground & slept like rocks, & did not wake til morning, much refreshed this was the hardest march we have had, we came 11 miles, this place is called Edray.

Sunday, August 4th, 1861, Diary Entry

Our waggons arrive this morning, they stayed on the road all night, being too dark to proceed there is a very fine spring here so we are taking good rest.

Monday, August 5th, 1861, Diary Entry

We left Edray at 10 1/2 o'c. I was in the vanguard, we had a mountain to ascend 4 miles called Elk Mt the road was quite rough, we reached Big Spring 17 miles, a little before the Regt which came up about 7 o'c there is the most magnificent spring I ever saw, gushing out of the rocks like a torrent as cool as possible.

Tuesday, August 6th, 1861, Diary Entry

Left Big Spring at 10 minutes after 9 o'c & trudged up the mountain 4 miles in very good time, now 11 o'c we are on quite a high Mt. with a very fine view we have quite a respectable force here, the enemy are said to be in 10 or 12 miles of us in strong force, we have about 8000 men around about us & more on the way. Genl Lee & General Loring are here. Loring lost his left Arm in Mexico.[11]

Friday, August 9th, 1861, Diary Entry

We went out on Picket last night, about 6 o'c with 60 men about 2 miles, Kept the main body in a house on the roadside & posted sentinels down the road but saw "Nary Yank" & returned this morning rather tired & sleepy, guard duty comes quite hard on us there are a great many sick in the other companies, we have 20 & sometimes more on duty at once.

William Wing Loring had lost an arm due to injuries suffered during the Mexican-American War. He commanded the Confederate Army of Northwest Virginia and got along poorly with Stonewall Jackson.
https://www.floridamemory.com/items/show/1668

Saturday, August 10th, 1861, Diary Entry

I just been relieved from Guard at Genl Loring's Quarters, now 11 1/2 should have been relieved at 9. It rained nearly all night & this morning, we staid in an Ambulance to protect us from the rain. It is very monotonous here. It rains nearly all the time & Picket duty very heavy.

Tuesday, August 20th, 1861, Diary Entry

Major Ship[12] came to us and ordered us to get ready for a scout 11 1/2 on Sunday night the 18th we marched to the rendezvous but did not get off till 10 o'c 300 men in all commanded by Col Langhorn[13] of the 42. It started to rain soon after we started. When we had gone about 7 miles over the roughest road I ever laid foot on, we came on a Picket & were very near firing into them they were so frightened that they could not answer our challenge. We kept on & came to a house where the Col supposed we would find a party of Yanks. We double quicked through a field of grass & surrounded the house. We were wet through by the grass up to our waists.

Major Scott Shipp served as major of the 21st Virginia Infantry Regiment until January 1862.
Library of Congress Prints and Photographs Division,
https://lccn.loc.gov/2016646226

We broke in & searched the place, but found no one the remains of a meal was on the table. We kept on, trying to catch up with them as every [sign] looked like they had just left we came to another house & another double quick, but they were not there. It was now broad day, we were hungry as wolves & very tired, after going 10 or 12 miles we divided into different parties. I in one of 25 led by Lieut Welford, with guides, we went up the mountain, there was no path right through the bushes, it was rough work, we finally reached the top & could see a picket in the valley beyond we were tired & some of the boys fell asleep leaning against the trees.

We started back & passed a house, where we engaged breakfast then 12 o'c we eat as only a hungry soldier can.[14] We had some excellent Potatoes, Corn bread, butter & milk. We had nothing but berries from the time we left until this breakfast I never enjoyed a meal so much this table looked quite desolate after we were through we rested awhile & returned to the place we left the other parties, while waiting, there came up a tremendous rain. It seemed as if the very floodgates of heaven were loosed it fell so hard as to be painful to the skin. It fell in sheets strait as an arrow, the others came up very soon & we started back, the rain had swollen the little streams so much that we could cross them only with great difficulty, there was great danger of being swept away, some had to run their bayonets in the ground to support them, we wet as man could well be from head to heels, boots full of water we crossed stream after stream for miles before we came to the main road, the men scattered for miles some nearly exhausted, the road was like a creek of mud & water. We struck out for camp on our own hook & arrived there about 8 o'c as forlorn a set of fellows as one need see tired, wet & muddy, & sleepy & hungry[15] I was the 1st one in the boys were uneasy about us, thinking we were lost or taken as soon as I arrived I threw off my wet clothes & put on dry ones & took a nap & something to eat & sweet were both. All the men that are able are on duty. I am on Camp Guard. I write this (Diary) on my knee in the guard tent. I stand it better than I expected. I washed my clothes the present day, greased my boots & cleaned my gun & am ready for anything that may come to pass, some did not arrive until quite late.

Thursday, August 22nd, 1861, Diary Entry

The boys on Picket have brought in 2 prisoners, about 10 miles from camp, they were captured.

Sunday, August 25th, 1861, Diary Entry

One of Mastine's[16] men died & was buried to-day it was a very sad affair, the 1st one man we had buried a very rough coffin was made, Geo Peterkin[17] read the service we having no Chaplin he was buried near the top of the mountain Col Gilham was present.

Requiscat in pace.

Sunday, September 1st, 1861, Diary Entry

Some of our men had a skirmish with the Yanks, a day or so ago, in which our guide was killed & 3 Yanks bit the dust or more likely "mud" & the remainder, some 30 or 40 ran, there is supposed to be some 5 or 600 of the rascals about 7 miles from us.[18]

A Tennessee Regt came to us very hastily supposing we were fighting. We had been firing off our guns they went up, to scout about, & saw some of the Yanks, but made no demonstration.[19] Another Regt has gone out to reinforce them & may have a fight.

The weather is delightful to-day. We gather the finest Blackberries I ever saw about the country, made some excellent pies to-day of them.

Sunday, September 8th, 1861, Diary Entry

We have orders to move to-morrow we are going to make an advance to-ward the Yanks, who are supposed in strong force near us.

Col & Mrs Fontaine have arrived to nurse Morris[20] who is very ill with the typhoid Fever she sleeps in the tent with him, she must have a very disagreeable time, they both came up on one horse. Peterkin nursed him before they came like a mother.

We buried a Lieut in Mustine's Co to-day named Hubbard,[21] the 4th man of the Co. We have a great many sick in the regt. We left John

Worsham, John Powell, & Dick MacMurdo in Huntersville when we left, also Jesse Child, they are recovering.[22]

Richard MacMurdo of F Company.
Chamberlayne, *Ham Chamberlayne, Virginian*

Tuesday, September 10th, 1861, Diary Entry

We left camp yesterday about 6 1/4 o'c P.M. & bade adieu to Valley Mt. for time. We marched 3 1/2 miles & bivouacked in an old shack, the rain very heavy. Col Gilham told the F & B that Genl Lee told him he must take care of us, that he valued us as much as any Regt, quite a compliment.

We heard a great deal of firing ahead during the night, but could not find out the reason of it in a skirmish yesterday, our men killed 2 or 3 of the enemy. We lost no one.

We obeyed the order to pack up with alacrity, as we were all tired of doing no thing but Piquet & guard. We left our sick in camp with their tents. We left our Mess Chests behind.

Wednesday, September 11th, 1861, Diary Entry

Started yesterday morning on our march, after a cold breakfast, from our sacks, but advanced very slowly. We countermarched, placed ambushes &c til we [were] tired enough. Capt C.[23] on a turn of the road, sent me, with 2 men to beat the bushes to see if any body was on our flank & got a lecture for exposing myself. We were finally posted on the road side for the night our Co was divided, one part under Lieut Mayo[24] took post on a side road, the other Capt Cunningham on the main road, as a picket, I was in the last We kept a lookout, but nothing happened except a little rain, it was so rocky on the Mountain side that we could scarcely lie down. We only came 4 miles that day.

Captain Richard H. Cunningham, Jr. led F Company.
Chamberlayne, *Ham Chamberlayne, Virginian*

Thursday, September 12th, 1861, Diary Entry

We marched off with the rest of the Regt yesterday morning, but advanced very slowly having to wait til a party who had gone around to intercept the picket could come up. We had gone about 1/2 a mile & having to wait a long time I with 4 men was sent to reconnoitre as soon as we appeared they opening on us when getting permission to fire we returned it & had quite a sharp skirmish for a little while, a spent buck shot struck John Reeve[25] in the stomach & a ball hit Sgt Pizzini on the foot but glanced. We at last threw off our knapsacks & charged down the hill. When they ran, the flanking party came in sight. We were near firing on them, some blood was seen in the mill where they were posted, one or two were killed as they ran by some of the flankers. We went back, to get our knapsacks & the regt moved on left in, they had a barracade in the road, which was removed. We passed the body of one fellow on the road, shot in the back of the head, he was a very large man & looked like a German, he was buried on the road side, some think 4 or 5 were killed.[26]

The Brigade was not to-gether, after going a short distance we came on the main picket a company or more, but they left in a hurry as soon as we came in sight. Lieut Welford Acting Quart, rode in a party of them, they fired but did not hit him, he fired his pistol they ran, the Companies in front picked up quite a lot of India Rubber cloths blankets, &c they left a quantity of meat, crackers cooking utensils &c. It has rained a good deal to-day, the country is much better than we have been in before, this is a beautiful Valley & the roads very good.

We went in as far as Conrad's & bivouaced in the woods, during the night it rained very hard, & we were completely drenched, & got up this morning cold & wet, but had to pack up   our Knapsacks were considerably heaving than yesterday, the order was countermanded however, & we were given permission to build fires, the first time since we left Valley Mt. We eat what remained in our sacks & dried ourselves & blankets & were quite comfortable.

We started again & advanced very slowly. Genl Loring & Staff were a head, the enemy fired some 300 odd rounds, a piece of Ga Artillery (Troop)[27] sent a shell at them & scattered them, the enemy answered with a shell. I saw it after wards, conical about 8 in long & 5 or 6 in diameter Col Washington was killed by venturing too far.[28] We were very anxious to charge the battery, but were ordered in the woods & some bread & meat came up for us. We left cooks at Conrad's, it was very acceptable, the firing soon ceased, about dark. We were ordered to take a position across the creek, called Tigerto valley river on the Mountain Side. Lieut Miller[29] was left with a squad in the field to look out. We came 2 miles to Crouch's.

Friday, September 13th, 1861, Diary Entry

We passed the night very comfortably. It was cold & damp & had to keep a lookout, & most of the men were wet crossing the creek in the morning the enemy fired on a picket ahead of us, & wounded several of them, they passed by us, one wound in Jaw, one in the thigh, one in Jaw & shoulder, one in neck, & another in neck & shoulder, none very badly, one had to have his arm amputated. We were sent some meat & bread, in 2 horse buckets, it was very acceptable though, very mean, but not enough of it.

Saturday, September 14th, 1861, Diary Entry

We were relieved last night about 8 o'c by Capt Robinson's Co[30] & came over to the woods, where we were yesterday, & found some beef & hard bread which went very well, though, we were as hungry as wolves. We spread out & slept like bricks.

It is reported that about 3000 Yanks, 3 months men will [re-enlist] today.[31] We have taken a captain & 70 men.

Sunday, September 15th, 1861, Diary Entry

I was on guard last night. Tom Ellet[32] was sent up the Mt. to a place where he could look down in their fortifications, about 10 or 11 o'c Major Ship came to me, & gave me orders to awaken every Captain at 3 o'c & tell each to get out their Co & fall in line on a road in the woods.

Just before the time it set in to rain, & dark as pitch. It was with great difficulty I could find the Companies, succeeded at last, though completely wet & in danger of break my neck in the woods. The Troop Artillery & Regulars fell back 1 1/2 o'c. We fell in line on the road & all the pickets supposed to be in, we left (2 men in Berkley's Co we left behind on post, one was taken & got back to us at Valley Mt, they were there 2 days) Tom Ellet's party was found with great difficulty & brought in. We were deployed as skirmishers, across a field where Beaf had been killed which emitted not a very agreeable odor, but we ordered in, & started back in the evening, we march quite late. It began to pour down in torrents & the road that was very good when we passed over, now was over our "Knees" in mud & we were soaked through & through by the rain we traveled on, the whole Command was completely disordered, we turned in a field & built fires with great difficulty, having to hold an oil cloth over it while building. It stopt raining at last, we were served some rotten beaf on the way. Genl Loring was cursing all the way most & all of us were as sullen & gloomy as possible our "Heaven, Hell or Baltimore" did not come to pass in any case.

We marched 6 miles.

Tuesday, September 17th, 1861, Diary Entry

We are back at Valley Mt. again. We left our bivouac in the morning, 8 o'c & after quite a hard pull we arrived, we had to stop very often going up, we as near used up as any set of fellows I care about seeing, but we were so hungry, we had to go cooking, after getting some eatibles & pitching our tent, we laid down, & slept, as only a tired soldier can long & sound & all up this morning as fresh as you please though stiff & rather footsore.

We marched 5 miles on the 16th & 4 on the 17th.

Sunday, September 21st, 1861, Diary Entry

I received a box from home, with my birth day cake &c in it (19th). We all receive a great many boxes &c from home, they come in good time for we are often without anything except Beaf & flour, neither Sugar, salt nor coffee & very often not full rations of that, we had a splendid dinner of Goose, Cake, Wine, ham &c it was a perfect feast.

Tuesday, September 24th, 1861, Diary Entry

Every thing is quiet nothing of any importance is going on, the sick are all being removed back, who did not leave before & preparations are being made to move back.

We struck our tents & pack up everything we could, had to burn Mess Chests, Camp Beds & all articles not absolutely necessary, we carried all our duds to the top of Middle Mt. It was very hard work, it was about 1 1/2 miles, we will move over this evening, or in order, we left at 5 1/2 & bade adieu to Valley Mt, I trust <u>forever</u>. We have suffered much & had but little pleasure on its muddy crest, all the others had gone we were the rear guard of that forlorn looking army.

Wednesday, September 25th, 1861, Diary Entry

We moved down to the foot of the mountain, carrying every thing on our backs, about a mile, we pitched our tents, having bivouaced last night, we found a good many blackberries.

Friday, September 27th, 1861, Diary Entry

It is & has been raining in torrents since last night, we had no breakfast but something found in our haversacks, a picket came in this morning dripping wet. Dan Talley[33] went out on a forage & after going about 7 miles came in with some splendid Peaches, which we laid violent hands on & engaged most extravigantly. As we were all lying in our tent, to keep out of the rain we were ordered to "Arms" in consequence of one of our Pickets having been driven in by a party supposed to be in considerable force, we were soon ready, the Regulars went up the Mt. raining all the time, we were dismissed with orders to keep in readiness.

Sunday, September 29th, 1861, Diary Entry

It rain all day the 27th as we were keeping as comfortable as possible in our tent an order came to detail a Non-Com & 10 men for Picket. It being my turn, I rigged up but not with great glee as you may imagine, only 4 besides myself could be found to go. I reported to Capt Irving[34] he appointed my Orderly of the Picket, we trudged up Middle Mt. raining as usual, the road was a perfect river, had great difficulty in posting sentinels both on account of the Mud & darkness. I passed by one sentinel & he did not see me, a man could not see his hand before him. It rained all day, we got no sleep, but morning came at last,[35] sent 2 men to call in the outer pickets, we then set to work to destroy the stores & provisions &c some 10 or 15 bags of coffee, salt, flour, medical stores, 2 boxes of "wine" which was remarkably soon destroyed, tents, ammunition &c, the Pickets having come in & passed us, we started, when reached camp, or where it was, we found our knapsacks left on the ground for us, tents burning guns broken & such a scene of desolation as not often seen, we passed Big Spring, some 30 odd waggons were jammed together, & all kinds of baggage, trunks &c some guns were left loaded in the waggons, which exploded when the fire reach them, dead horses were numerous.

The streams were swollen into rivers rushing along like a charge of Cavalry, we were taken up to the thighs, so swift it was with difficulty we could cross, waggons & horses were jammed up in the drift where they had been washed, a complete wreck the horses & mules drowned & their contents washed away or smashed.

We continued our march, wading through water & mud as they came in order. I saw one fellow ride a poor horse who could scarcely walk across the stream & then shoot him down & put an end to his wretched life, horses were seen all along the road, rolled off the road in the mud at rest at last. The roads seemed to have no bottom in some places & it was with great labor we could get along, constantly crossing streams, we caught up with the Regt at 2 1/2 o'c where they had stopped to let the artillery get ahead, they moved so slow that we had quite a good rest, built a fire and dried ourselves.

We started again, but moved very slowly continually stopping. We built fires as evening came on being cool but would hardly have them going well before we would go a short distance farther & so on til near dark, when we started again, we passed over what could not be called a road because we could not walk in it, but very little, but had to take to the woods & make our way best we could. I had an axe in one hand & gun in the other, Knapsack on my back, it being dark. We stumbled along about 3/4 mile when we had to stop, we could go no further. Segt Ellet stuck in the mud & fell down covering himself from head to foot. Prvt Mohr[36] stuck so fast that he had to be pulled out, it was very dark, we built fires & bivouaced for the night the men were scattered all along the road, we suffered agony on that march. It was almost mechanical that I progressed at all, having no sleep the night before, on Picket. I laid down & slept, as you imagine a tired man could for one who has not tried it, has very little idea of it, we came about 5 1/2 miles.

Monday, September 30th, 1861, Diary Entry

We marched off very much refreshed by our nights rest, about 9 o'c but progressed very slowly, the men became very much scattered, so I struck out on my own hook, & reached Hogsett's where we bought a pig. Man Page, John Powell, Dr Coleman[37] & myself set to work, cleaned him but as we [were] going to cook it, we had to move off, so John & I slump it on a pole & started, we went as far as the foot of Elk Mt. & stopd the company soon came up we quartered Mr. Pig, had some bread & had quite a good "chaw."

We have not tents & cooking utensils are common property, we spread down by a good fire & had a glorious nights sleep, the [roads] are so bad that I can't find words to express how bad they are, no one who has not seen them can known what they are, one of the Regulars died on the way, we came about 5 miles, all very much used up.

Tuesday, October 1st, 1861, Diary Entry

We were ordered back to Hogsets, our Co & a N.C. Co on Picket about 3 miles, we are the outer pickets, on the 31st I had a flanking post with 9 men on the Mountain side, which I went up to look around, saw no one, but found some apples, which I brought down, to the boys. The other troops have gone to Elk Mt. to barracade the road, to prevent enemies coming, should they attempt it, we have 24 hours rations. The family of Hogsett have left bag & baggage, we cooked under difficulties having to bake bread in frying pans. Tom Ellet & I cooked for 8, this morning, some of the boys under Lieut Mayo, went back to guard a by road, we sent something to them I took a good wash in the branch this morning, had very little sleep.

Wednesday, October 2nd, 1861, Diary Entry

We have not been relieved yet. It rained a good deal to-day, we were relieved from our post & went to the house for our Knapsacks &c wet. Capt C. myself & several others went to the house, made some bread & coffee & had a very Fair breakfast, we have used up all our provisions We dried our fixings & clothes & under the circumstances & placed felt very comfortable, it was very cold last night & night before, we found our overcoats very comfortable.

3 o'c we are on duty again with a very promising chance of remaining another night. We have had to eat Pumpkins roasted, corn or anything we could find it has stopd raining fortunately, but looks <u>damp</u> overhead. I went out on a little scout, as one of the boys thought he saw a horseman I saw nothing however.

Thursday, October 3rd, 1861, Diary Entry

We were relieved about 6 o'c last night but it being too late & road almost unpassable, we remained til morning, & for the 1st time slept in a house all night, up stairs we left in morning at 6 o'c & reached camp after a hard pull of 6 miles, we were out the whole time on 24 hours rations, there is no need of saying anything about the road except it is as bad as it can well be. We reached camp at 1/4 to 10 o'c we stopped 4 or 5 times to rest, the party with Lieut Mayo arrived last night, the troop are felling trees & blocking up the road, our tents are on the roadside, our boys were here who left Valley Mt. with the sick, they gave us something to eat.

Friday, October 4th, 1861, Diary Entry

We have moved our camp to the top of Elk Mt. We did not pitch our tents of which we have 7 now, saved from the wreck but slept by fires. I wrote home by Paul, C. A. Robinson left for Richmond,[38] news has just arrived that Jackson has gained a victory at Greenbrier River, our loss was slight but the enemies very heavy, a complete rout.[39]

It took place yesterday.

Sunday, October 6th, 1861, Diary Entry

3 of the Pawnees myself among the number started out on a foraging expedition.[40] We obtained a pass & struck out to Moores where we engaged 2 bushels of Potatoes, we then headed for the Mountains it was rough traveling, we came to a house, but could get nothing there, so we kept on about 3 miles came to a fine peach orchard, the trees bending down with the fruit. We eat as many as we wanted & bought 2 bush. for $100. We went a little farther & got a very good dinner coming back we filled our haversacks, but they would not hold them. Wm Exall[41] pulled off his drawers & tying up the legs filled them slinging our loads we started back.

I killed a very large black snake coming with my pistol. We passed it on the way back we had hard work as it was up hill nearly all the way & very rough but we finally arrived at the top of the Mt. puffing & blowing, but such a magnificent view expanded before us that we quite forgot our loads, we could see for miles & miles, Mountains on Mountains, the trees all of changing colors under the last rays of the sun & thick forest was most beautiful, the Greenbrier winding among the Mountains like a thread, it was glorious, but we had to leave & soon arrived at camp &

threw off our delicious load, which gladdened the hearts of the Mess they dived into them with great gusto, we had eaten so much that it greatly impeded our progress, but the exertion gave us a little more space so we could not help eating a few.

Wednesday, October 9th, 1861, Diary Entry

We received a good many boxes a day or two ago, so we have a large addition to our baggage, so of course we move. We cooked last night our rations for to-day. I was on guard last night, we move early, packed up & carried every thing to the top of the road to be hauled down to Edray, we had to carry them about 3/4 mile, quite hard work. We had only some 4 or 5 waggons for the brigade.

We took an-other view from the Mt It is magnificent. We "F" are waiting for the order to move, are last as usual, all the others are gone, this is one of the prettiest camping grounds we ever had, the woods are all changing & the leaves dropping, warning us we had better be leaving. When we arrived at the top we saw how little transportation there was, we each took something in our hands & started down to Edray. 4 1/2 miles we passed some 4 or more graves of our men who had died there, the place looked very desolate & lonely, our camp is about 1/2 mile from the old one.

Friday, October 11th, 1861, Diary Entry

Some of us went out on a forage, killed a ground hog on the way, had a very [rough] road to travel. We went over a mountain, jumping from tree to tree where they have been felled for some purpose. We came to several houses, obtained by a little persuasion & money some butter, chestnuts, Peaches, Apples, & a little Maple Sugar, saw a very nice looking young lady named Rosser who seemed to be of rather a better class than most of the country people, we had quite a lively chat with her, we returned to camp at 2 o'c.

Saturday, October 12th, 1861, Diary Entry

We went out again to-day & secured some butter &c have issued to us to-day for rations Sugar & Coffee, the 1st we have had for some time, the sugar is very poor, but not enough of that.

Sunday, October 13th, 1861, Diary Entry

A courier came to Col Gilham that Rosencrantz[42] was retreating & Lee had taken some horses &c. We are living very well now, any quantity of fruit by paying a good price for it, we are all getting fat, there is scarcely a man who can button his coat. We have orders to move at 7 o'c in the morning to Greenbrier Bridge.

Monday, October 14th, 1861, Diary Entry

We are all ready to move, packed the waggons &c but did not get off [until] about 9 o'c. We had quite a heavy frost this morning. We reached the Bridge about 3 o'c, we had to stop frequently as the waggons stalled & had to be unloaded. We crossed the River & went up the bank about 1/2 mile & camped, it is a very pretty valley but our ground is rather damp. We came about 4 miles, our waggons having come up, we laid off camp & pitched tents in order once more.

Tuesday, October 15th, 1861, Diary Entry

We had a heavy frost, but not quite so heavy as yesterday. We passed over part of the road, we had such a good time on the night of 3rd Aug, under rather different circumstances. I recollect well a drink of white whiskey I had, then we rested at the bridge on the 3rd, it refreshed me wonderfully, we cut down the wild grass with swords to put in our tents, it is very pleasant to lie on.

Friday, October 18th, 1861, Diary Entry

It rained a little last night. John Powell & Myself slept under a fly, the tent being crowded. It is quite comfortable & more healthy than a tent. We have made a bed of small poles covered with hay.

It is reported that Jackson's Pickets have been driven in, have drill at 1 o'c now.

Friday, October 25th, 1861, Diary Entry

We have Sugar to-day 19th [October] 1st time since the 12th our rations very irregular, we had a little snow the 24th, it was very cold, winter is coming fast, hard frost & Ice this morning, looks threatening over-head. Genl Anderson's Brigade[43] passed us to-day. Col Patton[44] & Capt Paxton Quart.[45] arrived this morning. Paul came also. Genl Loring is here.

I think Loring's prediction will come true as there is good foundation we will winter here, if we do, Heaven or Hell will have the greater portion, & some may get to Baltimore, if they are taken prisoners.[46]

Sunday, October 27th, 1861, Diary Entry

I am on Guard at Genl Lorings Quarters. I write this in Col C. L. Stevenson's tent,[47] who very kindly gave us the use of it. I received a box yesterday, we had no rations this morning & no salt for several days "there is something rotten in Denmark,"[48] the Commissary department is very badly managed & the Quartermaster is equally bad.

Wednesday, October 30th, 1861, Diary Entry

This morning a young deer came near Camp, I suppose from curiosity, there was a general rush to "Arms" several shots were fired at it, it was struck but traveled up the mountain remarkably fast. I fired as it was running, but think missed it, a guard was immediately ordered out, we were arrested & I was confined to my tent. Lieut Hancock also, others put in the guard house. [49] We have an inspection & muster for pay to-morrow, it is blowing hard & cool.

Friday, November 1st, 1861, Diary Entry

I was released yesterday morning. We were inspected & mustered. It was a very tedious job, our camp was also inspected. It was very cold last night. Ice quite thick. We just came off drill, we had quite an amusing scene after drill. Tabb[50] & Col [illegible] not very proficient in drill were taken out & put through by Sgt Rawlings,[51] the maneuvers were amusing in the extreme, they were very much ashamed at it.

Saturday, November 2nd, 1861, Diary Entry

It rained very hard last night & this morning our tents & ground was flooded, we had to set to work & dig a ditch to the river & drain them.

Sunday, November 3rd, 1861, Diary Entry

It snowed a little last night & this morning we are just off inspection, as usual on Sundays, we have no flour, it is frequently the case we don't get our rations at the proper time.

Tuesday, November 5th, 1861, Diary Entry

I left camp yesterday for 48 hour picket. We are on the outpost on Elk Mt. about 8 miles from camp, our position was decided in the very military style of "Tossing up cents" instead of being assigned by the Officer of the day, but things are managed here very much in that way, the most of the Officers are perfectly ignorant of their duties, & some, very much "big" as the darkey says,[52] one actually washed in the stream where we get our drinking water, & on being ordered by the sentinel to desist, said he was an Officer & priviledged to-do it, but the sentinel soon proved him otherwise.

It was very cold last night & windy. We are in an old Log house, which protects us some, there is a good deal of snow on the mountain & very cold. We had quite a hard tramp up here. It is so cold that the men have to stand 1/2 hours instead of 2 hours, the wind blows great guns here, has a clear sweep at us. I have charge of the outpost.

Letter, Tuesday, November 5th, 1861

Camp about 3 miles from Staunton
November 5th, 1861

Dear Pa,

We arrived here last night about 8 1/2 o'c after a very cold ride on open Flats[53] of 3 hours & a half, the cold was so intense that the boys built fires in their ovens to keep warm we had quite a fall of snow on the 2nd I had the pleasure of being "on guard" at the time the weather had been very cold, the water freezing on our hair before we could wipe it off, our boots frozen when we get up, but we don't seem to comprehend how cold it really is. We have become inured to it, we, as usual, left very suddenly & had to wait about 2 hours in the cold at the depot for the mail train, like all our movements, done in a bungling way.

We suppose from rumor that we will be ordered to the Eastern Shore, but I don't think anybody here knows anything about it. Have you had a pair of boots made for me yet. these I have are nearly used up send them to Staunton.

I wrote from Milboro & Telegraphed here hope you received them. We can feel the change in the atmosphere very sensibly, it is warm enough without a coat though snow is on the ground yet while at Milboro, we required an overcoat to be comfortable. We suffered a great deal coming down, I think I never was so cold for a short time in my life. You had better direct your letters to Staunton & they will be forward to us. We are all well hope you all the same at home write soon.

The things in the box for Dr Crump I had no means of getting them to him so we appropriated them, the bundle for Tho. Frayser, I sent by one of our boys to the Rock Alum to Mr Frayser who will get it to her the other for Mann Page & Wambersie[54] I delivered, many thanks for the box & Potatoes, my best love to all.

Your Affectionate Son,

Tucker

Wednesday, November 6th, 1861, Diary Entry

It has been raining, hailing, or snowing the whole time we were on picket, except a few short intervals. We got something to eat at Gay's near us, bought some apples, the officer of the guard went out on a scout yesterday but saw nothing of the Yanks.

Some of the Regulars shot one of Gay's sheep they were arrested.

We were relieved at 1/4 to 2 o'c the cold was intense we started back Bob White & myself started back & walked very rapidly, reached camp in 2 hours, raining all the time, it is 10 minutes to 4, the roads are very muddy. We were very wet when we arrived.

The Vote to-day was for Tyler 22, Lyons 19 & MacFarlane 2.[55]

Friday, December 6th, 1861, Diary Entry

The weather is quite warm & pleasant.

We are not allowed in town (Staunton) at present, some of the Fs were arrested yesterday for running the Blockade.

Saturday, December 7th, 1861, Diary Entry

We held an election today for junior 2nd. Most of the boys held a caucus last night, the candidates were W. G. Gray, J. B. Payne, and C. R. Skinner.[56] Gray received the Majority of votes, so he was the Candidate. John A. Pizzini 1st Sergt was opposed to him. Gray received 52 votes Pizzini 15.

Our orders are very strict about going to Town, a guard is sent in to arrest all found there. 4 from each Co are allowed to go in.

Wednesday, December 11th, 1861, Diary Entry

No one is allowed to go to Staunton without a written permission from Col Gilham, but numbers run the blockade, the Guards have a hot time running down their game much to the delight of the boys & Ladies, it looks rather ridiculous. The weather is quite warm, but looks much like rain. I heard Dr. Sparrow (Episcopal) on Sunday,[57] was rather disappointed, a great many pretty girls in Staunton, saw Mrs. Tyler from Richmond, paid a visit to the Lunatic Asylum with some of the boys.[58]

Letter, Wednesday, December 11th, 1861

Camp near Staunton
December 11th, 1861

Dear Pa,
Your letter of the 29th Nov & 9th Dec are both to hand.
I am very sorry to hear Ma is so unwell hope she will be better soon. I have not received <u>one</u> of the papers you sent. Where do you direct them? I tried to get a pair of boots in Staunton but could not but bought a pair from one of our boys, they not suiting him, I don't know what he paid for them, but he will find out soon. I drew (15) dollars from Mr. Cowen.
Capt Cunningham wrote at my request to Col August.[59] I know it would be best to be a Commission Officer but <u>if</u> he has a vacancy in any one of his companies, an Adjutant could be appointable as being an Officer in the Co.
We are all well, the weather is very mild & pleasant but looks like rain. We elected a Lieut in Henry Millers place. Mr. G. Gray received 52 votes & John Pizzini 15.[60] Lieut Mayo's resignation has been accepted, so we have to elect another.
No one is allowed to go to Staunton except by written permission of Col Gilham, the town is under Martial Law. My best love to all.
Tell Peyton to write me, hope Ma will be well soon.
Your Affectionate Son,
Tucker

Letter, Friday, December 13th, 1861

Staunton
December 13th, 1861

Dear Pa,

I am at present on guard here, the town is under Martial Law. Capt Clarke[61] Co B is Provost Martial. We are put to some expense, as we board at the Hotel the place we are given plank huts very uncomfortable, & no accommodations for cooking so we are forced to stay here.

The weather has turned very cold & we will see a very hard time if we go to Winchester, which seems very likely all the troops have been taken from the line we have been operating on. Gen Loring has issued orders not to allow any person to leave in the direction of Richmond without a permit from himself except civilians. We take possession of the cars every morning & stand duty about the place all day to suppress any disorder &c a very unpleasant duty.

I bought a pair of Boots from one of our boys for 9 dollars not very good but the best I could do, there is a great demand for Boots & shoes here the Factory is working very hard but cannot supply the demand.

I hope Ma has recovered from her sickness, & that all are well at home, write soon we are all well, give my best love to all & yourself among the rest.

You Affectionate Son,
Tucker
Tell Peyton he must write me.

Saturday, December 14th, 1861, Diary Entry

I am established ere (Staunton) on the Provost Martial Guard since Thursday 7th. Capt Clarke Co B is Provost, with 24 men the place has become very quiet. We, that is the Fs & Bs have a room at the American didn't like things at the Virginia. Capt Cunningham brought the Pay Role for us to sign last night. I went out to camp & received the [illegible] for myself & the other boys in town, had numerous commissions for the Camp boys, as we are not going with them. The Regt came through town in fine order followed by the 7th Tenn, the Ladies were out in full force, they took the Winchester turnpike, the first the Regt has left me behind & I didn't like it much. I have forgotten to mention that D. D. Talley Wm Exall & Myself became acquainted with the Misses Braxton from Fredericksburg staying at the Rev Mr Taylors,[62] two very pleasant young ladies. Miss Fanny is the youngest but I like Miss Lizzie better. I also visited with Ritchie Green[63] the Misses Peyton who I had seen in Richmond at the Exchange.

It is very dull lounging about with nothing to do.

Wednesday, December 18th, 1861, Diary Entry

Last night about 1 o'c we discovered a fire near us, so slipping in our Pants & boots we ran down to it & found the Confederate Stables in a blaze. We pitched in & worked like turks, the firemen did not seem to be very efficient. We saved a part of the building & some carriages & stages but a large number of the best horses were burnt. Genl Loring lost 1 or 2, some say 50 or more horses were lost. I rode Capt C's mare & rode all about looking out for the stray horses, got to bed about 4 o'c very nearly played out & wet, it was hot work, as we had to use buckets.

Letter, Wednesday, December 18th, 1861

Staunton
December [*18th*] 1861

Dear Pa,
Yours of the 16th is to hand with the check enclosed. I paid Mr Corsan the 382. I have plenty of money now. I suppose you received my letter with the checks & money.

We had a very large fire last night, or rather this morning, at about 1 o'c we were awaked, & jumping in my boots & pants I made for it & found it was the Confederate Stables. We worked like Turks & succeeded after almost superhuman efforts in saving about a 1/3 of the buildings, but lost some 50 or 60 of the finest horses in the country among them Genl Loring's We save Capt Cunningham's, the firemen are not worth their salt. We that is the guard with some of the citizens did all the work. I worked with some of our boys on the sheds until it became so hot we could not stand it but saved the shed & most of the wagons &c. The remains of the poor horses was awfull. I worked until I was wet & completely exhausted & hoarse & rode all over the place hunting horses till about 4 oc this morning & went to bed & the way I did sleep is a caution "To all who go to bed early & get up late."

We hear that England has demand the unconditional surrender of Mason & Slidell.[64]

All well, my best love to all.

Ever Your Affectionate Son,

Tucker

Friday, December 20th, 1861, Diary Entry

We have had quite a gay time in our room lately. Egg Nog &c &c party of visitors. We carried Col. Hansbury[65] from the cars to the Virginia on a litter, wounded in the thigh.

Friday, December 20th, 1861, Pocket Diary Entry

We have had a "tremendous" time this evening. Egg nog &c &c several guests we carried Col Hansbury to the Virginia wounded in the thigh.

Monday, December 23rd, 1861, Pocket Diary Entry

Left Staunton on 22 at 8 o'c & arrived at Strasburg after a long ride & raining about 11 1/2 o'c. staid in the Hotel till this morning when after several attempts found our camp about 7 o'c. It is very cold, trip cost 4.25

Wednesday, December 25th, 1861, Pocket Diary Entry

We received our Sibley[66] Blankets & shirts yesterday. We are all packed up ready to move, the wind blew like a tempest night before last, most of all our tents were blown down, made up bread left camp near Strasburg about 1/4 past 11 & made 11 miles over a very fine road by 3 1/2 near New Town. Stevensburg, passed 25 odd waggons with Iron from the Baltimore & Ohio road.

Friday, December 27th, 1861, Pocket Diary Entry

Had all packed ready to leave but had to wait sometime before we left & marched over a fine road through Winchester support arms looked very well, our co in front, were received with waved handkerchiefs &c we are encamped about 3 miles from Winchester, marched about 14 miles.

Sunday, December 28th, 1861, Pocket Diary Entry

Was on guard last night very cold. had an election Welford was elected 1st & Payne jr. 2nd.[67]

Letter, Monday, December 30th, 1861

Camp near Winchester
December 30th, 1861

Dear Pa,

I wrote you from Strasburg & here, but have received no answer. I suppose you have received them by this time I have been expecting an answer about the "Requisition." I have been to Col Gilham several times but he says he has [not] seen or heard of it. I asked in my last whether it was sent to Col Gilham or Genl Loring. I think it would be well to send me a duplicate.

We have just been through a Brigade Inspection & Review. Col Gilham, his brigade is composed of our Regt. Col Burke's 42nd & Col

Campbell's 48th,[68] the Regular Battalion & Marye's Battery[69] estimated about 2200 men. We have an Inspection to morrow for Pay.

Reports are very contradictory as to our movements, some think we go to Romney, others to Martinsburg & on to Maryland, but I think it is too late in the season for that, some day we will winter somewhere about here.

I hope you all enjoyed a merry Christmas. I took mine on the road, had some Mince Pie last night which J. N. Parker brought to John Worsham.[70] Saw Jack Ellerson[71] day before yesterday. I suppose Hailie is at home now give my love to her. Hoping you are well & expecting an early answer with much love to all,

I Am Your Affectionate Son,
Tucker

Tuesday, December 31st, 1861, Pocket Diary Entry

Had Brigade Inspection & Review yesterday, looked very well, & a Regimental Inspection Muster this morning. We leave to-morrow morning have orders to cook 2 days rations.

Letter, Tuesday, December 31st, 1861

Camp near Winchester
December 31st, 1861

Dear Ma,

I wrote to Pa yesterday. I drop you a few lines to let you all know we leave tomorrow morning for (we all suppose) Romney, where Gen. Kelley is supposed to have some 15000 "Yanks" advancing this way,[72] so there is yet a chance for the "F" to mingle in the exciting & deadly combat which we no doubt they will do to their credit – We had an Inspection & Muster this morning & are all ready to do our countrys bidding to the best of our ability. I have no doubt but that we will whip them as we have quite a large force of Militia who had done good here before, & the troops in the division are almost Veteran in the hardship of the Campaign. Gen.

Jackson Brigade is the finest in the service, all are equipped & armed with Enfield & Mississippi Rifles,[73] also Pendleton's & Shumaker's celebrated Batteries.[74]

Direct your letters <u>Via Winchester</u> they will be forwarded do some of you write. I have not received a single letter since we left Staunton, have not heard from the <u>Requisition</u> yet.

Hope you have recovered from your attack & that all are well at home my very best love to all I am well & healthy, write soon.

Ever Your Devoted Son,

Tucker

4

From Romney to Kernstown
January to March 1862

Under the command of Stonewall Jackson, the 21st Virginia Infantry embarked on a winter campaign against Union forces in northwestern Virginia.

As the New Year approached, Maj. Gen. Thomas J. "Stonewall" Jackson feared that multiple Union armies would combine and then move on Winchester, Virginia, at the head of the Valley. Jackson resolved to move first and disrupt Union plans. He thought that a winter attack on Romney would allow the Confederacy to collect resources from the Kanawha Valley and protect western Virginia from Union forces. Jackson's men, concentrated around Winchester, would move on Bath and then head to Romney.

Unfortunately for the Confederates, winter weather hampered the campaign. Marked by privation and bitter cold, Jackson's campaign to capture Romney ended in ignominious failure. Controversy over the campaign prompted Jackson to tender his resignation, though he later withdrew it.[1]

Wednesday, January 1st, 1862, Pocket Diary Entry

Camp No 1
New Years day left camp Mason about 7 o'c & reached our camp 10 miles about 3 o'c it is very windy.

Wednesday, January 1st, 1862, Diary Entry

Were aroused this morn at 3 o'c & left our camp about 7 o'c & advanced very slowly, stopping about every 15 or 20 minutes, it was very cold, but built fires along the road, the road in some places is very bad, we camped about 5 1/2 o'c, a mile from water. Our waggons stuck in the mud. Now 10 o'c with nothing to eat & no blankets, it is very cold we made about 12 miles.
Camp No 2

Friday, January 3rd, 1862 and Saturday, January 4th, 1862,
Diary Entries

We left camp rather late & advanced very slowly when we came suddenly on a scouting party of the Yanks. Old Stonewall, in the lead. Col. Gilham came to us & Co. B & sent us up in the road, where we were loading amidst quite a scene of confusion caused by the scampering of the horsemen. Wm Exall was shot in the leg above the knee & was taken off to a house. Col. Patton's horse was slightly wounded. We deployed in the woods & returned their fire, killing 4 or 5 & wounding several. Lieut Payne was shot in the neck, the enemy ran & we bivuaked, for the night went on Piquet early in the morning, it commenced snowing early in the night. Col Barton lost his horse.[2] Wm Exall's leg was amputated but he has since died. Payne's is critical yet hears of his arms being paralyzed.[3]
We left camp this morning about 3 or 4 miles from Bath. We advanced very slowly, & very cold, throwing out Skirmishers, the enemy fired several shells and Minnie Balls, but we advanced & sending Cavalry in front who charge at full speed & run them out but they gave a volley to no effect, took 7 or 8 prisoners, also 8 at our 1st Muss[4] they were good

looking men. We passed double quick through Bath, on our way to Sir John's Run but darkness came on us about a mile from it, the enemy were in sight but we drew back, & are now bivuaked. We have been very highly complimented by the Generals & men in the division the General saying he never saw troops so cool in his life who had not been under fire before.[5] The enemy has 1500 men in Bath & several cannon.

After winning acclaim at the battle of Manassas,
Confederate general Thomas Jonathan "Stonewall" Jackson
led an ill-fated winter campaign in Western Virginia.
Library of Congress Prints and Photographs Division,
https://www.loc.gov/pictures/item/2011661081/

Monday, January 6th, 1862, Diary Entry

We left our camp near Sir John's Run & after numerous countermarches on different roads we have at last struck the road to Hancock. We are about 3 miles from it, & are camped it snowed all last night Col Rust was ambushed with the Danville Artillery but by his presence of mind he saved it, but lost 8 or 10 men.[6] Gen Jack was also ambushed but got out safe Col Stevenson said he would rather command the 21st than any regt. in the service, our Co has received numerous compliments.[7] We are in sight of Maryland, the enemy spiked 2 guns.[8]

Thursday, January 7th, 1862, Diary Entry

We marched down near the River & stayed some time, & marched back, moved our guns in position but fire but little, the enemy fired several times killing & wounding several, got a good many overcoats &c.

Wednesday, January 8th, 1862, Diary Entry

We were aroused by Reveille at 3 1/2 & packed up everything but had to wait until near 1 o'c for all the waggons to pass which took near 4 hours, the roads are slippery as glass with ice & cold as it well could be. We moved very slowly & made Bath after dark when we pushed forward slipping all the way some of the men injured themselves very much one broke a leg another his thigh, the horses fell continually artillery had to be pushed. Ice formed on mens bears from their breath in a solid sheet the streams bore men. We arrived at our waggons some 16 or 18 miles about 11 o'clock with out stopping, spreading out we slept only as soldiers can sleep.

Regts were mingled to-gether in utter confusion, it was like a stampede, burnt the Depot & secured a good many stores.

Thursday, January 9th, 1862, Diary Entry

We packed up & after some difficulty with the waggons arrived here (Cross Roads) after dark & pitched our tents it rained a little. We are now awaiting orders, wrote home this morning.

Friday, January 10th, 1862, Diary Entry

We have just been to bid farewell to Col Gilham and Major Ship[9] the company presented the Col with a horse yesterday cost 250$ with "here's your mule."[10]

Letter, Sunday, January 12th, 1862

Camp in Morgan Co
January 12th, 1862

Dear Pa,
I wrote Ma a letter a day or two ago in answer to hers of the 5th & sent it by Major Ship, who with Col Gilham left us to go back to the Institute, the company made him a present of a horse, cost 250$ we were very sore to part with them as they with us.

Genl Jackson is granting furloughs to the No of 4 or 5 to each company for 20 days. I sent in an application, but as there are some 25 to 30 applicants, those who have the most pressing business are granted first, as I have no business at all & considering the No of applicants I think there is very little chance for me, still I may get one some time or other.[11] We will no doubt go to Winchester in a day or two & then they may extend the no of each company & if so I stand a very good chance, as Lieut W[12] who is in command (Capt C.[13] being in command of the Regt. Col Patton being on furlough) says he will give me one when all those who have pressing business have received theirs, but even in that case it will be some time yet.

The weather has turned quite mild but in consequence of the snow melting & a little rain the roads are horrible. Write soon.

I am well & hope you are all well at home, my very best love to all, yourself & Ma.

Ever Your Affectionate Son,
Tucker

Monday, January 13th, 1862, Pocket Diary Entry

We have done nothing until this morning, when we were aroused before day & packed up, but on account of the roads which are very bad, we only came about 200 yards & are now camped in sight of our old camp, it is very cold, have orders to move to-morrow morning, had a ration of whiskey served to us.

Tuesday, January 14th, 1862, Pocket Diary Entry

It snowed all last night we are now pack up ready to move (10 o'c) not quite so cold as yesterday had a ration of whiskey this morning. We started about 11 o'c each Co with its waggons & arrived at our camp about 8 miles after a hard time having to push our waggons all the way. We arrived about 7 o'c but had to cook, are at it now, <u>11 1/2 o'c</u>, it was very cold, our horses very nearly played out have orders to move at 6 o'c with 2 days cooked rations.

Wednesday, January 15th, 1862, Pocket Diary Entry

Left campo about 11 o'c & after a good deal of trouble, & our waggon upsetting we made abt 5 miles by 5 o'c.

Thursday, January 16th, 1862, Pocket Diary Entry

Left camp & tramped down to the River, but it had risen & washed the bridges away so we had to cross on horses waggons & in one small boat it took us some time & as the road was quite slippery we picked it & pushed the waggons & in that way go along pretty well, camped quite late having made about 7 miles.

Saturday, January 18th, 1862, Pocket Diary Entry

Left our camp where an Old Camp Meeting place was at 7 o'c & after quite a hard march & good deal of difficulty with the waggons. We are now about 3 miles from Romney, marched near 12 miles through quite a fine country saw 5 or 6 houses that the Yanks had burned & a very large Tannery, it has been snowing or hailing nearly all the time.

Monday, January 19th, 1862, Pocket Diary Entry

We were given rations of Butter taken from the Yanks & crackers, it has been raining all night and nearly all day most of the snow has disappeared.

Letter, Monday, January 19th, 1862

Camp near Romney
January 19th, 1862

Dear Pa,
Yours of the 9th in the bundle by Geo Peterkin is safe to hand, many thanks to Ma and yourself for both. I am surprized you have not received my letters from Morgan before this, but hope you have by this time. The socks were just in time, as marching over this rough country plays the deuce with a fellows <u>under</u> <u>gearing</u>.

Mail communications are very uncertain now, so you must not expect many letters. I don't know now how I am to get this off, but trust to chance.

I suppose you have heard ere this of Romney being in our possession. The Yanks left in such a hurry that they left some of their provisions & burnt some tents, this is a great achievement for if they had stood it would have cost the life of many a brave fellow before we could have taken it, they were quite strongly entrenched. The weather has laid up a good portion of our command. When we left Winchester, Jackson had about 12,000 men, now he can scarcely muster 7 or 8,000, one Regt from Ga started with over 600, now they have about 150.[14] We have as large a no as any Regt here, but can only no about 350 or 400, all the men have very bad colds. I have gotten along very well with only a slight cold, which is much better.[15]

Have you had much bad weather in Richmond. You write such short epistles that I can get no news of how things are at home. I know you are busy all the time, but Ma or Norman or some of you who have time ought to write me Letters in camp are great things to pass time. It has been raining all day & last night, most of the snow has disappeared, & it is much milder.

It is probable that we will stay here some time as some troops will be here all the time but no one knows which division it will be, and it is just as probable that we will tramp off to some place that no one but Old Jack knows anything of, he has the faculty of keeping his plans to himself in a perfect degree, even Genl Loring second in command did not know we were coming here.

It is a very general impression in camp that Genl McClellan is waiting until the 12 months enlistment of our troops expires, when unless some expedient is adopted our army will be very much disorganized, & then make a grand swoop down on all sides of us, in consequence the department has issued a circular to all troops now in the field who will re-enlist for 2 years, a bounty of 50$ & 60 days furlough, they are privelidged to elect their own officers & choose their arm of the service, & I suppose if the war ends before the 2 years are out they will be released. I expect that the next enlistments will be for 2 years at any rate, so I am in doubt to which I will do, whether wait until my time [is] out & take the chance of getting home or take the bounty & furlough now.[16] I may get a commission but if I do not I am hooked for two years, but if go home the 21st of April I take the chance of being drafted in the militia. What do you think of it, the best thing would be to get detailed to Richmond during the winter and then I could see about some better arrangement. If on the 21st of April some great move should be made & we expect a great struggle in the spring, we could not leave just when we are needed, and I think the greater portion of our boys will stay, if such is the case.[17]

Let me know what you think of it, write soon my very best love to all. I am very well except a slight cold. Hoping you are all well.

I am Ever Your Devoted Son,

Tucker

Tell Mrs. Tompkins that Ned is well[18]

Friday, January 24th, 1862, Pocket Diary Entry

Left our camp about 3 1/2 miles from Romney about 10 1/2 & are now quartered in the Bank.[19] It is snowing hard we had rain or hail nearly all the time we were in camp, our cavalry had a little skirmish, both ran no one hurt

Saturday, January 25th, 1862, Pocket Diary Entry

It commenced snowing yesterday & continued all night. I am on guard.

Thursday, January 30th, 1862, Pocket Diary Entry

We were aroused this morning at 2 1/2 with order to pack up we loaded the waggons but have not done any thing. It snowed quite fast to-day, numerous reports have been going the rounds all day.

Saturday, February 1st, 1862, Pocket Diary Entry

There was a duel on the "tapis" yesterday between Capt Jones & Lieut White, weapons Guns loaded with bucks, 30 paces, a large scouting party went out this morning, a Regular gave 20 dolls for 2 canteens of Ka whisky.[20]

Tuesday, February 4th, 1862, Pocket Diary Entry

We received orders on the 2nd & to take 24 hours rations, our waggons left on the eve of the 2nd but we did not get off till the next day about 2 o'c, it was snowing very hard, & blowing in our faces. We met our waggon about 8 miles mired. We stayed with it, but had to stop about 10 o'c the horses having give out we built fires & stayed on the road all night. We worked very hard to unload once we left about 6 1/2 & after numerous halts reached camp 18 miles about 12 o'c we then we ordered to cook 24 hours rations & be ready to march to Capon bridge by sunset, 5 miles which latter was countermanded, so we are preparing to bivuak for the night. The Tennesseans burnt all their camp equipages. We lost 2 waggons, the snow was about 6 in deep. We passed numerous houses burnt on the road by the Yanks, the burnt Bluis & an old cobbler in his house, the road was very rough.[21]

Wednesday, February 5th, 1862, Pocket Diary Entry

It was very cold last night, the coldest we had had, had to get up about 3 in the morning. We packed up & left at 8 o'c & after quite a hard march of about 12 miles which we made by 2 o'c we camped Ernold & Hodson 2 of Bs died a day or two ago, were carried to Winchester.[22]

Thursday, February 6th, 1862, Pocket Diary Entry

We brought in 6 men & 1 Corpl I being in command, yesterday evening. We got up about 4 this morning & left at 7 I was on the waggon guard & after quite a hard time we reach our old camp about 3 miles from Winchester by 12 1/2, much milder. It hailed or rained nearly all the time we were on the road.

Saturday, February 8th, 1862, Pocket Diary Entry

We went in to Town yesterday to escort the remains of Ernold and Hodson Dr. Quintard officiated,[23] bought a pair of boots for 15.00

Letter, Saturday, February 8th, 1862

Winchester
February 8th, 1862

Dear Pa,

I have <u>just</u> received your letter of the 27th & have been wondering what was the matter than some of you did not write. I have not received the socks nor the letter by Robinson.[24] You <u>know</u> how much I <u>wish</u> to come down home, but <u>sooner</u> [stay] than come as <u>some</u> <u>do</u>. I would stay the 12 mos out, for a good many as you say have no more business than I do but resort <u>to</u> <u>dishonorable</u> <u>means</u> <u>of</u> <u>getting</u> <u>them</u> <u>&</u> <u>that</u> <u>I</u> <u>do</u> <u>not</u> <u>mean</u> <u>to</u> <u>do</u> but I will try at once to get a furlough, for I assure you I wish to <u>come</u> as much as you all do for me. I have not <u>made</u> any engagements I don't see any chances to <u>make</u> any <u>here</u>. My very best love to all. I am well. Hoping this to find you all well.

I am Ever Your Devoted Son,
Tucker

Letter, Sunday, February 9th, 1862

Camp 3 Miles from Winchester
February 9th, 1862

Dear Pa,

I wrote you yesterday in answer to yours of the 27th which I had just received. We reached here several days ago, after going through almost incredible fatigues & cold. We had one heavy fall of snow, about 6 inches, & either snow or hail nearly all the time we were out. I suppose you have heard of our leaving Romney to its fate, the command is nearly used up by the severe weather we had. 2 Baltimorreans died on the road from Pneumonia,[25] & most all our boys are suffering from Rheumatic afflictions. Genl Loring left for Richmond this morning to try & get authority to grant furloughs to nearly all his command, for an order had just been received to grant <u>no</u> furloughs <u>except</u> <u>to</u> <u>those</u> <u>who</u> <u>will</u> <u>re-enlist</u>

for 2 years. That I don't mean to do, yet, for I want to get out of this Army & to get in an Artillery Co. if possible as that is the easiest & best Arm of the service & one in which a man can make himself most noticed & I believe they get better paid. I am of the same opinion as you all, that one year is long enough to serve as a private, & I shall try all I can to get a position this year. Gen Loring says he can't expect this Co to re-enlist as privates but that we ought to be looked to for officers. He has a very high opinion of us, you say I can get a commission without doubt? do you know of any opportunity now for one, or do you only suppose that because there will be an entire change of Co that I may be able to get one? The Commission of Wambersie I understand from one of his own Co amounts to nothing, as I said in my last letter I am anxious to get a furlough as any one, but there are men in our Co now who have applications signed by the Co & Regt Officers who are married men & have business, all the passes are nearly at stake & Gen Loring wont sign them. I know there are a great many who get off one from our CO who passed on another mans pass & such dishonorable means which men of any honor or principle would scorn to stoop to. I, sooner than do it in that way, will stay till my time is out. I intended to go to Gen Loring this morning but heard he had started for Richd, though I think there is very little chance still I will do all I can do to get one. Tell Ma it certainly is not because I don't want to come home, but I have seen so many from our Co fail who I know have good & urgent reasons. Jos Willis[26] tried repeatedly although his mother was dying it was only after the urgent interference of Dr Coleman[27] that he got off in time to see his Mother die. Do you see it is no easy matter. We are anxiously awaiting for Gen Loring to return to see what is to be done with us.

I will write as soon as I can learn anything. Write me often. I am thank God well as ever in spite of all the hardships we have been through, hoping this to find all well & with much love to all.

I Remain Ever Your Devoted Son,

Tucker

Genl Jackson has a great load on his shoulders to answer for in this Campaign.[28]

Letter, Monday, February 10th, 1862

Camp near Winchester
February 10th, 1862

Dear Pa,

Yours of the 30th with Harlin's and Norman's reached me yesterday. I acknowledged the receipt of the Books &c from Romney & supposed you received it. Did you get a letter from Peyton Johnson?

Re-enlistments are going on very <u>rapidly</u> here. I write now to ask you what you think of the proposition. If I enlist for 2 years, I receive 50 dollars & 30 days furlough <u>at</u> <u>home</u>. I have the privilege of selecting any <u>Co</u> or <u>Arm</u> of service & electing my officers or of getting a commission myself. On the other hand, if I <u>don't</u> enlist my name will be given to the Commissioner & subject to <u>draft</u> of course those who enlist will have the preference of furlough & those who don't will stand a very bad chance indeed, <u>do you think I could get a commission in 30 days</u> if I were to be in Richmond because if I don't do it in 30 days I will have to join the best Co I can as a private. I will do whatever you say but the opinion here is very much in favor of the 2 years scheme, of course if the war is over before the time is out we will be released. <u>Please let me know as soon as possible</u>, give my very best regards to Mrs Paul. I will answer Harlin & Norman soon. Much love to all & hoping all are well. Write soon.

Ever Your Affectionate Son,
Tucker

Monday, February 17th, 1862, Pocket Diary Entry

It is very cold & raining it freezes as it falls.

Letter, Monday, February 17th, 1862

Camp near Winchester
February 17th, 1862
Dear Pa,

I have just written you a letter when I received yours of the 14th to let you know that we are all ordered to <u>Manassas</u> & <u>expect</u> to move tomorrow, but as no "<u>positive</u>" <u>orders</u> have come yet, direct here, when we move I will let you know where we are.

Your idea of re-enlisting is exactly mine, as there is not much chance for <u>many</u> of <u>our</u> Co re-enlisting at <u>present</u> they wish to change their Co & get out of the North-West, most of them desire to enter the Artillery Service & believe all will go in service again for all of us feel that there will be a tremendous struggle this spring & the Old Dominion will need every arm that can wield a weapon. I intend to offer mine as long as it can obey my will. The 50$ <u>was</u> no inducement whatever, but I was only anxious to get <u>home</u> & the furlough was the principal inducement, but the time short now & I can very easily "bide my time" for furloughs to <u>well</u> men are almost out of the question the command is too much reduced now.

I suppose you have read the "bill" about drafting <u>if</u> I should be drafted (for I stand a <u>chance</u>) the best I could do would be to get in the best company I could find but if I get off I will come home if possible when my time is out.

Give my kindest regards to John Cor & tell him to write me.

Why does not ma write something. I hope she is well, my best love to her.

Is there any chance to get in the Marine Corps, if so let me know. Please send me 10$ we have not been paid off yet & I am broke "intirely." The weather is cold & rainy my best love to all the home folks write soon. I am very well.

Ever Your Devoted Son,
Tucker

P.S. We get the <u>paper</u> <u>here</u> so you had better not send any more. Is it true that Genl Loring is under arrest in Richmond.[29]

The order to move has been countermanded for the present.

Letter, Sunday, February 23rd, 1862

Camp near Winchester
February 23rd, 1862

Dear Ma,

Your letter of the 15th reached me yesterday after taking a trip to Clarke Co. having been sent to the family of Dr. Robert G. Randolph by mistake. This is the 1st letter I have from you for a long time. I thought you must be sick but Pa never mentioned it. I have just received Pa's letter of the 21st, with the 10$ enclosed for which I am much obliged. I will look out for the bundle. I have plenty of socks shirts & have 2 under shirts & 1 pair drawers bundled up to send home with Bob White directed to Ellet & Weiseiger & will send it by 1st opportunity.

Genl Jackson has issued orders to allow <u>no</u> furloughs. By reenlisting one can get the 50$ but <u>not</u> the furlough the command is so much reduced that <u>not</u> <u>a</u> <u>man</u> can be spared but when we get to <u>Manassas</u> there may be some chance to get the furlough which we expect every day.

There is quite an effort here to keep up the Co. as we all find it would be too bad to allow old "F" to sink into oblivion, some wish to change it into an Artillery, the Capt to keep in the Infantry, but it will soon be decided what we will do & I will let you know.

I <u>think</u> I might be able to get a Com in some company if I were in Richmond but a company could not be <u>even</u> <u>uniformed</u> for 500$ besides I don't care to put Pa to the expense of it, if I can't get a commission[30] I can go in again as I am now. I am no better than a <u>great</u> many others who are serving their country as <u>privates</u>, but of <u>course</u> if I can <u>better</u> myself I will do it, so I think I had better wait before I do anything <u>final</u>. In the mean time if you see any opening for me you can let me know (<u>Is</u> <u>there</u> <u>any</u> <u>opening</u> <u>in</u> <u>the</u> <u>Marine</u> <u>Corps</u>). Thomas Ellet has written to Richd to get an explanation of the Laws relating to re-enlisting & drafting.[31] I fear that just about the time we are out of service there will be the greatest need for us & that a great many will not be able to get home at all, as soon as we get to Manassas, I will do my best to get a furlough, even for a few days, so look out for any chance for me in Ricd. I will do my best for <u>myself</u> here if the Company is reformed. We have some rumors of the fight in Mo but as yet nothing definite. Remember me to all the Cowardin family & my best respects to Miss Alice, tell Jack he must write to me & tell me what he means to do.

I assure you that <u>you in</u> a house mind the weather more than <u>we</u> who are <u>out</u> in it. We are in some measure like the Indians now don't <u>mind</u> anything except orders from our superiors. God has spared me through such trials as I never expect to see again & I trust he will spare me through those to come. I have seen <u>every</u> feature of a soldiers life except a <u>regular</u> battle, more men are killed by disease than the sword[32] & I am in perfect <u>health</u> so I think I will get through safe with the protection of our Holy Mother.

Give my best love to all the servants. I hope I may soon be able to do it myself. I long to take old Dash[33] in my arms once more before the old fellow dies, hoping this to find you all well & with much love to all.

I Remain Ever Your Devoted Son,

Tucker

Monday, February 24th, 1862, Pocket Diary Entry

We have had a tremendous storm of hail of wind which leveled nearly all our tents & some trees & quite cool.

Thursday, February 27th, 1862, Pocket Diary Entry

We received orders at 9 o'c last night to cook & leave by Day, this morning Reveile beat at 3 o'c we left abt 8 1/4 & marched abt 5 miles & are now encamped 2 miles from town. It is quite cool, had a very little snow.

Letter, Saturday, March 1st, 1862

Camp near Winchester
March 1st, 1862

Dear Pa,

The bundle came to hand yesterday all safe. <u>Many</u> thanks to <u>yourself</u> & <u>Ma</u> for the shirt, socks, books, &c. I do not need the shirt <u>yet</u> as these I have are good so you had better not send the other. I have no means of carrying them.

We have moved our camp from the Romney road to the Berryville road. We are expecting reinforcements from Manassas. I don't know <u>where</u> or <u>when</u> we are going. I should not be surprized if the Yanks should attempt to take this place but think with reinforcements we can hold it. It is the key to the whole valley & must be held at any hazard.

Have you received my letters from here, the last I wrote to ask <u>you</u> <u>to</u> <u>see</u> <u>if</u> <u>you</u> <u>could</u> <u>not</u> <u>get</u> <u>me</u> <u>a</u> <u>sergeantry</u> in Mr. Crenshaw's Battery.[34] It is the best thing I can do unless I can get a commission which I don't see any chance for now.

I have never received the letter with the medal Ma mentions.

I know you must be very busy, so I don't expect <u>you</u> to write so often but Ma is not busy nor Norman & they must write oftener. It will be good for Norman's hand.

The weather is very windy & cold. We had quite a hurricane the other day, which leveled near all our tents & several trees but fortunately hurt no one.

This act of re-enlisting gives the men in the field no chance whatever. We who came at the first call & have stood the storm for 12 months, are put in a worse position than those who staid at home while we were braving everything & <u>now</u> when they will be forced to it stood to <u>raising</u> companies & come in the field as officers, while the men who <u>know</u> & <u>have</u> <u>experience</u> serve as privates & the <u>numskulls</u> as officers. If a man re-enlists he can't get a furlough nor <u>can</u> he change his <u>company</u> <u>Arm</u> & <u>Division</u> so says Genl Jackson & from the <u>act</u> we all think as he does.[35] It is doing justice to the men, if those who are afraid to brave the timid field had some out as men, we could have driven the cowardly vandals from our soil before they could have gotten such foothold, but I must close, as the mail leaves. I will write again soon, much love to all I am very well. Write soon & let me know of the Battery.

Ever Your Devoted Son,
Tucker

Letter, Thursday, March 6th, 1862

Camp near Winchester
March 6th, 1862

Dear Pa,

I wrote yesterday & enclosed 50$ of my pay, hope you will get it safe. I rec'd the Song Book.

I have promised to go with Capt Cunningham, who is going to Richmond to reenlist. He says he would like to have me for one of his Lieuts but of course he can make no promises, but I stand a very good chance. Geo Peterkin & some of our <u>best</u> men have gone with him. I see nothing better. He goes to Rich tomorrow I <u>may</u> get home on the recruiting service with him but don't know yet. I write to let you know. It is the best & only thing I can do for a few days we will <u>have</u> to say whether or not we <u>re-enlist or not</u> & are subject to draft. I think it is a disgrace for anyone like myself who has nothing to keep him out of the field to hold back & be <u>forced</u> to fight for his country & this I never intend to do. It shall never be said that <u>I</u> was <u>drafted in the Militia</u>.

I have thought over it for some time & have come to this conclusion. What do you think of it? Write soon. Love to all. I am well.

Ever Your Devoted Son,
Tucker

Saturday, March 8th, 1862, Pocket Diary Entry

Went on Picket yesterday snowed & rained nearly all day & night, raining now Dr. Coleman & Col P arrived. Were paid off, sent 50$ home.

Saturday, March 8th, 1862, Pocket Diary Entry

We have just returned from Picket, our camp has been moved 2 miles below Winchester. We heard firing all day yesterday caused by our cavalry firing on 2 Regts of Infantry 2 pieces of artillery & 1 Co Cavalry of the enemies. They fired their Guns very often at our Cavalry but they fell back to Bunker's Hill 7 miles from us. We were 5 miles from town. We took 3 or 4 fine horses & killed several more & wounded several of the Yanks. One of our Cavalry was wounded in our breast. We were ordered back to town, the outer picket under Sgt. Gibson[36] fell back soon after the firing commenced 2 miles leaving us exposed, when near 2 miles from town Capt. Irving ordered us back. It was then dark, we went back and were relieved today. We passed the Regt in town going out to the Martinsbr road, the Brigade went to pull down the fences &c in the neighborhood. Some of Ashby's Cavalry on the Berryville road killed 4 & took 6 prisoners.

Wednesday, March 12th, 1862, Pocket Diary Entry

We moved from our camp 2 miles from W. yesterday morning, & passed through town on the Berryville road, & drew up in line of Battle, but were ordered to the Martinsbg road where we also drew up in line but in a short time were ordered to support Pendleton Battery on a hill to our left.[37] We went up & built fires it now being dusk, but had been there a very short time when we were ordered back to overtake our waggons, (The Picket which left the same morning was driven in wounding a horse & men it is supposed our boys killed one of the Yanks) which we did abt 9 mi 1/2 o'c. 5 miles from Winchester, we were ordered to cook but we laid down under a stone wall & went to sleep having no wood near to make fires we roused up this morning at daybreak & after a very hot & fatiguing march are camped about a mile from Strasburg. It was very hard to give up the place, the Ladies waved their handkerchiefs when we went out, but when we came back all was dark & silent, those few we saw were many in tears. We have it is thought about 5000.

Thursday, March 13th, 1862, Pocket Diary Entry

We were ordered to load the waggons but kept our tent, abt 10 1/2 o'c we were aroused & ordered to strike tents & pack up. We laid down by the fire without cover.

Friday, March 14th, 1862, Pocket Diary Entry

Ashby had a skirmish & drove them in a mile of W.[38] have orders to leave at 7 o'c I & Geo Peterkin were elected Sgts yesterday.

Saturday, March 15th, 1862, Pocket Diary Entry

We packed up this morning & left at 8 o'c soon after we left it started to rain & kept up all the way it rained quite hard & bids fair to continue all night. We are camped abt a mile from Woodstock 10 miles from our other camp.

Wednesday, March 19th, 1862, Pocket Diary Entry

Left camp abt 8 o'c & arrived near Mt. Jackson abt 2 o'c abt 11 miles we were rear guard.

Friday, March 21st, 1862, Pocket Diary Entry

Left camp abt 2 o'c and camped abt 4 1/2 coming abt 4 miles. It rained nearly all the way. It snowed & rained all night. We have orders to move at 7. It is snowing very hard.

Letter, Friday, March 21st, 1862

Camp near Mt Jackson
March 21st, 1862

Dear Pa,

I have not written before because I have been expecting a letter from you <u>every</u> day but have not received one since 1st March. I wrote on 5th & sent 50$ had you received it? I suppose you have heard of our retreat from Winchester. We are now about 50 miles from Staunton, the Yanks are said to have about 40,000 men our force will not reach 6000 but Old Jack takes his time. The whole retreat has been conducted with great coolness & decision we have not lost a single man or any stores whatever. We have made a clean sweep of all the Munitions of War (& there was a <u>very</u> large amount of them).[39]

The Militia are coming in quite strong. When we left Winchester we had about 5,000 we are gaining strength every day & with a little time we will be able to clean the Vagabonds out of the most beautiful part of the Old Dominion. We have orders to move back to-wards Strasburg for what purpose I don't know. The Yanks are said to be near Woodstock. Ashby the "Marion" of this war holds them in check with a few men,[40] we think Col E. Johnson with his Brigade from the Allighenies is coming to re-enforce us[41] you may expect to hear stirring news from this quarter soon, either of good or bad, for Jackson will never give up while there is a <u>shadow</u> of a chance, some of the boys ("F") had a little brush while on picket near Winchester, but none of them were hurt. I have been promoted to 3rd Sergeant, from 2nd Corpl. Geo Peterkin is 4th Sergt, some of you write soon. The mail is very much in disorder, direct to "Staunton to be forwarded" the boys are all well & "spiling" for a fight. Bob White & Ned Tompkins are well, write soon. My very best love to all at home.

Ever Your Devoted Son,
Tucker

Saturday, March 22nd, 1862, Pocket Diary Entry

It rained at intervals yesterday & last night but looks like clearing off. We are packed up to move 6 1/2, 6 was the time were to be in the road we left abt 20m to 9 & after a very hard march of 26 miles we reached camp abt 6 o'c, we have orders to leave at day break. We are abt 2 miles from Strasburg all the railroad bridges were burnt. Ashby killed & wounded abt 150 in his skirmish.[42]

A seasoned Confederate soldier of 1862.
Worsham, *One of Jackson's Foot Cavalry*

5
Kernstown
March 24 to April 9, 1862

Union forces under Maj. Gen. James Shields pushed up the Shenandoah Valley and had occupied Winchester. Jackson, commanding only around 3500 men, sought to turn back the approximately 7,000 or so men in Shields's division. On the morning of 23 March, Jackson's men advanced from Strasburg. Finding a Union force in his front and thinking he outnumbered it, Jackson attacked. Unfortunately for Jackson, he was mistaken. Initially, the Confederate line held, but then buckled under Union pressure and retreated.[1] Tucker would be wounded in this engagement, the battle of Kernstown.

Monday, March 24th, 1862, Pocket Diary Entry

We left our camp near Strasburg abt 6 o'c & after getting to New Town we heard guns ahead & came up soon after with the troop ahead, after waiting awhile we were ordered to support Pendleton Battery. We passed over a field & the enemy opening on us the shells fell thick &

near, part of one knocked Picot down.[2] When we got in our position, the Batteries opened & a brisk fire was kept up for some time, the enemy came up in some force to flank our batteries when we engaged them & kept them back for some time. I was struck in the foot & stomach, & left the field caught a horse let a Lieut get up behind me, soon after got up behind a Cavalryman named Eulks, he took me to Mrs. Rhodes where I was very kindly treated, & am now waiting to get to S. had my wound dressed Dr. Fleming came this morning.[3] Some 10 or 12 of our boys were wounded or killed.

Letter, Monday March 24th, 1862

Mount Jackson
March 24th, 1862

Dear Pa,

On the event of the [illegible] while on the way to Winchester & near Kern's Town, 2 miles from Winchester, we were ordered to support Pendleton's Artillery when the enemy attempted to Flank us. We received them warmly & the action commenced in earnest. The Yanks brought up fresh men continually, but we kept them at bay, for a long time. I was struck in the foot, but my boot turned it making only a bruise. When I had shot nearly all my cartridges away, I was struck in the stomach, & thought at first I was all used up. I got to the rear & had my wound examined. I found, It was only a flesh wound. The ball which was a minnie struck obliquely & came out on a line with my hip, passing between the outer muscles & the abdominals the wound is painful thought not at all dangerous & with time & good mending I will be on my [illegible] soon. If you have time I would like for <u>you</u> to come <u>but</u> <u>don't</u> <u>let</u> <u>Ma</u> <u>under</u> <u>any</u> <u>consideration</u>. I think if you will come up you can get me home. You can come to Staunton & take the <u>Stage</u> here. We may be moved back to Harrisonburg, you can enquire, the army is moving back, I don't know how far. We have 10 or 12 wounded none dangerously, Bob White & Ned Tompkins are safe. It is almost miraculous how we escaped being under a cross fire, come up if you can, I am getting on finely. John Worsham is waiting for me,[4] our mail is very much disordered. I have not had a letter since we were at Winchester, my very vest love to all at home & hoping this will find you all well.

I Am Ever Your Devoted Son,

Tucker

Tuesday, March 25th, 1862, Pocket Diary Entry

An ambulance came up to Mrs. Rhoades, Dr. Coleman with it. I was put in with Lieut Weaver.[5] John Worsham took good care of me.[6] I had to lay on my back. We came on to Mt Jackson, from Middle Town, 32 miles we arrived here abt 12 o'c at night we have abt 10 killed & 20 odd wounded we suffered intensely from the ride. Jackson said it was the hottest fire he ever saw, in the Regt. I am in a small room with 2 wounded men. We heard heavy firing from Cedar Creek when we were a short distance from Strasburg,[7] the 21st & Taliaferro Regt[8] were first engaged.

Wednesday, March 26th, 1862, Pocket Diary Entry

We were moved from the Hospital yesterday & stopped on the road abt 9 miles from Mt. Jackson, where we were treated very kindly & left this morning abt 7 o'c & came 22 miles to Mt. Crawford.

Thursday, March 27th, 1862, Pocket Diary Entry

Left Mr Myers at 7 1/2 & after quite a rough ride of 17 miles reached Staunton and are staying at Rev. Mr. Taylor's. Charlie is here. Telegraphed home.

Friday, March 28th, 1862, Pocket Diary Entry

Dr. Waddill came to see us yesterday, all the sick & wounded are coming in, a great many telegrams have come, about the boys. No train came yesterday we have all the papers to carry us to Richd.

Sunday, March 30th, 1862, Pocket Diary Entry

We left very suddenly & got on the cars, met Pa at Gordonsville. It rained & snowed nearly all the way got to Richd at 8 o'c left station at 10 had a great many to greet me, came up in the carriage to Mr. Purcell's, stayed all night.

Monday, March 31st, 1862, Pocket Diary Entry

Had a good many to see me yesterday. Slept very badly. It rained yesterday. We left in the carriage and arrived here at 6 o', came very slowly.

Tuesday, April 1st, 1862, Pocket Diary Entry

Did not sleep very well took some Laundanum.

Wednesday, April 9th, 1862, Pocket Diary Entry

Received a letter from Geo Peterkin a day or two ago, answered it. It has been raining for several days at intervals a great many troops &c have passed over the York road my wound is getting on very well does not pain me much. Great victory in Mississippi, Genl Johnson killed, no particulars yet.[9]

6

At Home
April to August 1862

Tucker's activities between April and September of 1862 remain largely unknown. As his diary entries make clear, his father took him from Gordonsville back to Richmond to recuperate.

Once well enough, Tucker continued his efforts to become an officer. He placed advertisements in the Richmond newspapers seeking men to join a new artillery company. If Tucker could get enough men to enlist, he could secure himself a commission as commander of the battery. Despite his advertisements for men to serve a battery of breech-loading rifled guns, for service with General John B. Floyd's division of Virginia militia, Tucker evidently failed to get enough men to enlist.[1]

Summer 1862 was a moment of great excitement for Confederates in the West. Defeat at Shiloh in April resulted in the Confederates falling back under Union pressure. The Union juggernaut pushed the Confederates south and out of Corinth, Mississippi. But at that point, the Union army stalled. Confederate General Braxton Bragg, commander of the major largest Confederate field army in the West, seized the opportunity. He aimed to defend Chattanooga, Tennessee against the

Union forces menacing it. He would also cooperate with the army of Major General Edmund Kirby Smith, then in East Tennessee. By the summer of 1862, Bragg and Kirby Smith had determined to take the war to the enemy; they would work together and invade Kentucky.[2]

When Tucker's letters resume in September 1862, they find him in an entirely different theater of the war and arm of the service. Instead of the infantry, Tucker rode with the cavalry. How Tucker secured that spot with Col. Henry Marshall Ashby remains unknown, or even why Tucker went out west. The letters below suggest that Tucker may have known Confederate general Henry M. Heth or someone on Heth's staff. Using that connection, Tucker might have ridden along as a volunteer, hoping that his skills might be recognized, and his position made permanent. In any event, Tucker evidently came to know Col. Ashby and joined his staff.

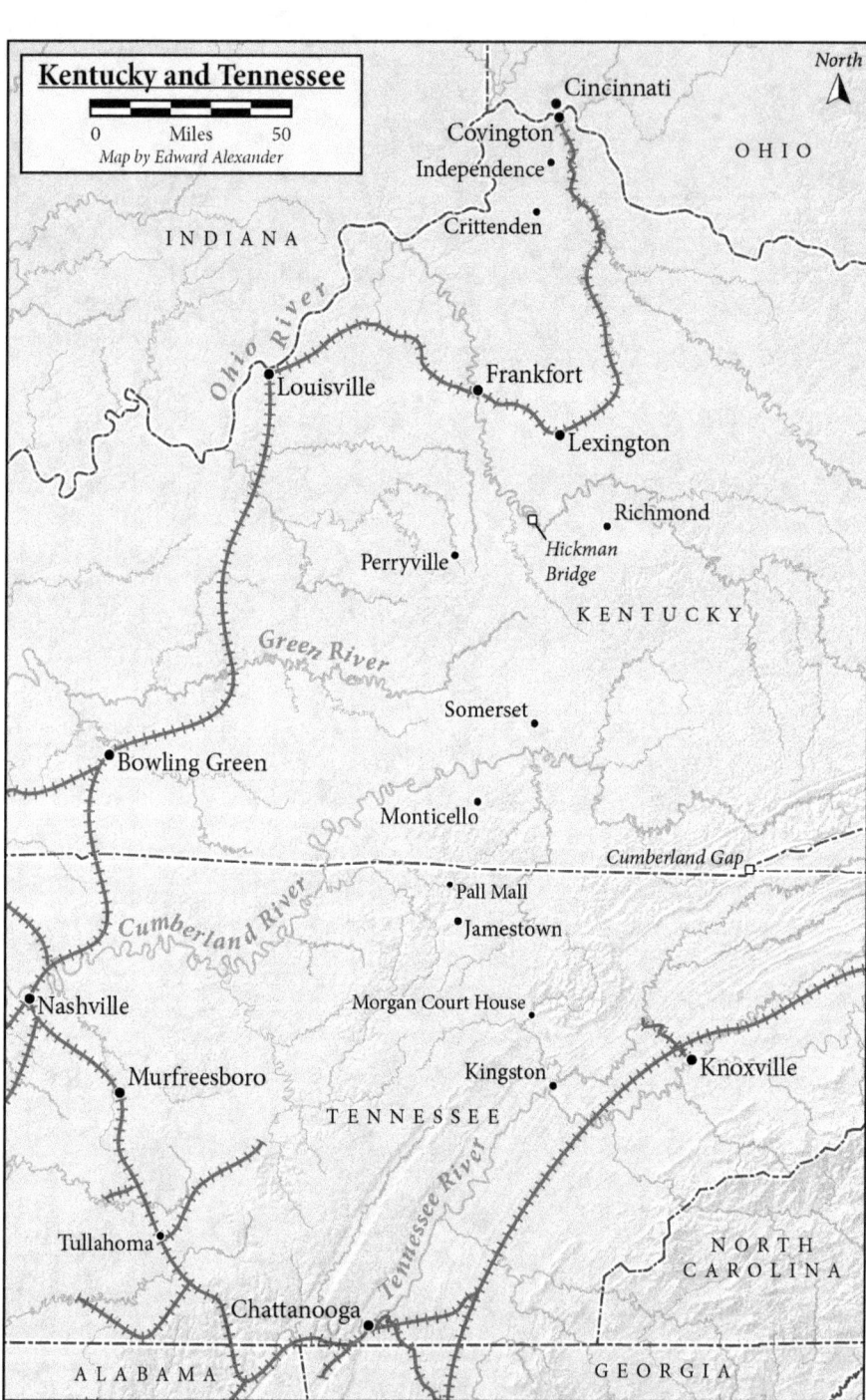

Kentucky and Tennessee

0   Miles   50
Map by Edward Alexander

OHIO

INDIANA

Cincinnati
Covington
Independence
Crittenden

Ohio River

Louisville

Frankfort
Lexington

Richmond

□ *Hickman Bridge*

Perryville

KENTUCKY

Green River

Somerset

Bowling Green

Monticello

Cumberland Gap □

Cumberland River

Pall Mall
Jamestown

Morgan Court House

Nashville

Murfreesboro

Kingston

Knoxville

TENNESSEE

Tennessee River

Tullahoma

NORTH CAROLINA

Chattanooga

ALABAMA

GEORGIA

7

With the Cavalry in the West
September to December 1862

Tucker rode as part of the cavalry under Kirby Smith. At the start of August, Kirby Smith set out from East Tennessee into Kentucky. Resolving to push through the mountainous regions of Kentucky—which could not support a major field army—Kirby Smith continued into the central part of the state. Union forces in the area gave disjointed response to the Confederate invasion from East Tennessee, and on August 30, Kirby Smith won an important victory at Richmond, Kentucky. While the Confederates and Union troops stood evenly matched, Kirby Smith routed his opponents. The Union lost more than 5,000 men (out of the 6,500 engaged) whereas Kirby Smith lost about 450 (out of around 6,500 engaged).[1]

Letter, Monday, September 1st, 1862

Richmond, Kentucky
September 1st, 1862

Dear Pa,

We arrived here this morning with Genl Heth who we have been with for some days as body guard.[2] We took this town after quite a lively fight in which the Yanks were completely demoralized some 3200 prisoners were taken, 6 pieces of Artillery, and 5 or 600 at the <u>lowest</u> calculation killed & wounded besides a large quantity of munitions of war, our loss will <u>probably</u> amount to 500, no more I think. The prisoners were all Paroled, except some few who had been Paroled before, who I expect will be shot. We are advancing on Lexington, will be there in a day or two. Genl Manson second in command of the Yankee force was taken. I saw him today. Genl Nelson (in command) was wounded in the thigh but I believe escaped.[3] Genl McRae of Texas is <u>reported</u> killed[4] & Genl Clairborne of Arkansas wounded.[5] It is reported that we have taken 1100 prisoners at the Kentucky River today 7 miles from this place.

Kirby Smith is in command here. Heth second in command.

This is quite a pretty little town & seems to do some business. There is a McAdams-ized road, quite refreshing after crossing the Mountains, this is quite a fine Country & well cultivated.

Will hear from me again soon. My best love to all relations & friends hope this finds you all well.

Your Devoted Son,
Tucker

Letter, Tuesday, September 30th, 1862

Lexington, Kentucky
September 30th, 1862

Dear Pa,

I wrote you from Richmond, Ky some time since and have not had the opportunity to write till now as we have been on the move continually and besides having all our communication <u>south</u> cut off but since Morgan has left the Gap[6] we can once more relieve the anxiety of our friends & relations as to our safety. I know you must be very anxious about me & I have tried repeatedly to get a letter through but so far without success. We are continually on the move scarcely resting a day going night & day but have been with Genl Heth from Va since we have been in these regions as a body guard, besides acting as scouts, we have had several little brushes with the Yankees, one near Independence (near Covington) in which we took the Flag from the Court House but were chased by about 100 Yankee Cavalry (we had only 25 men) for a mile or so when we turned in a bye road & fought them for a little while killing 3 & wounding one or two when finding we were flanked we fell back bringing the Flag in to Genl Heth, they killed one of our horses but did no further damage, my horse became perfectly unmanageable from the firing, but I stuck to him. I could use no pistol on account though I was near enough. My horse is a Yankee, & has been slightly wounded once so he is very shy, but am getting him jaded now from hard riding.

On the 17th we went down to Falmouth from near Crittenden & burnt the rail road bridge with 50 men took 5 prisoners, fought about 100 home guards, killing 3. We lost 2 killed & 3 wounded besides 4 or 5 horses, the enemy were in two large brick houses so had the advantage of us, Capt Ratcliff's horse was killed. We had to leave for fear of being cut off.

We are called the "Brigands" here & but few of our number can whip us.

We scouted in 1/2 a mile of the intrenchments in Covington in sight of the enemy on the breastworks. the enemy are very cowardly here in fact a great many of their men are "pressed" & won't fight. We have taken about <u>2700</u> prisoners since we have been in Kentucky. We have a large army here & recruits coming in every day. We <u>can't</u> be <u>whipped</u>. all our news from the east is encouraging.

The enemy is about used up in Kentucky. I don't think we will have any fighting of any consequence except perhaps at Louisville, which I hope to go to soon & call on Cousin James Cray.

You need be in no fear of my safety. I will look out for <u>No 1</u>. I am not at all to be buried in Kentucky or any other place at present but be assured I will do my duty whatever may be the <u>consequences</u>.

I often wonder how you are all coming on at home write first chance you find to care of Gen H. Heth. Ran Finney his A.G.[7] will give it to me to tell me how matters stand in Old Virginny. the more I am away from the Old Dominion, the more I long to see here again the Greatest & Noblest state on the Continent. Wherever you go, Virginia is held up as a noble example & her sons are treated with respect.

Is Norman in service now?[8]

Remember me to all my relations & friends.

How is Ned Tompkins & the other F boys who were wounded?[9]

My very best wishes home to Ma, Harlin, Norman, Uncle Ward & family & all my relations.

I will write as often as I can find a chance to send a letter. I am as well as possible to be, hope you are all the same.

Ever Your Devoted Son,

Tucker

direct to Lexington Ky.

Letter, Thursday, October 16th, 1862

Camp near Big Hill
Madison Co. Ky
Headquarters Genl Heth
October 16th, 1862

Dear Pa,

I take this opportunity to write home, as a gentleman is going to Knoxville. I wrote from Lexington, and hope very much it has reached you, as I know you and Ma must be very anxious to hear of my where-a-bouts, and welfare. I learn that some of our men came from Knoxville with some letters from you to me, but were taken by <u>Bushwhackers</u> & had to destroy them. I am very anxious to hear from home, but there is no communication in our rear, except when a body of cavalry is sent with dispatches through.

We are on the retreat from Kentucky after raising up the expectations of the people, and making them believe that we were going to liberate them, and causing them to express their beliefs freely and receive our money. the Union men will cause the secession men to suffer very much on that account, the whole truth of the matter is, Bragg & Smith have been most shamefully <u>out-Generaled</u>, this army was in splendid condition, and anxious to fight but will be very much demoralized by this retreat. We are making for Cumberland Gap as fast as we can travel, leaving Kentucky entirely in the hands of the enemy.

The result of the fight at Perryville is still in the dark, though Bragg fought with only 17,000, 30,000 of Buell's men we took some prisoners & a few pieces of artillery. <u>Hardee</u> said it was the hardest fight he was ever in.[10] <u>We</u> were at Harrods-burg at the time.

The General sent me out several days ago with 50 men, to watch the movements of the enemy. We scouted for a while and came on Genl Wood's (Yankee) division,[11] of 10,000 men, who were making a forced reconnaissance, they advanced within 2 miles of our lines when night came on. We stood picket all night, the next morning I visited the outposts, and found that the enemy had fallen back during the night. I then started to follow up their rear and caught a party of Yanks, a Lieut and 4 men who had 7 of our men taking them to Harrodsburg. They belonged to the 1st Ohio Cavalry. We got 3 Sharpe's Rifles, 3 Colt's Navies, & sabers, horses &c., the Confederates were very glad I assure you to get off.[12] We have a very rough set of men & difficult to manage, but they make good fighters and that is all that can be said of them. I have been trying to get out of the Company, but have not been able to do so yet, the Capt and I don't get along very pleasantly to-gether, if you can find any-thing for me to do, in the field any-where, I would like to know. I don't think this Army will do much as long as Bragg & Smith have command of it. I would rather be in active service, than stationary, and in any branch except the Infantry, unless I can ride. I am so accustomed to riding that I can't walk with the same facility that I trotted after old Stonewall.

I think it probably that I may be able to get some other position here, don't make any mention of this, or put your-self in to any uneasiness. I am or aught to be able after the schooling I have received in service to take care of No 1, and besides I have a good many friends out here, so I think I shall be able to get along.

Is Norman in service now or not he had better wait a-while, and learn more.

Hope Ma & yourself are in good health I often wish we were all home again in peace give my best love to all relations & friends hoping this will reach you all well, and that we may soon meet.

I Remain Your Devoted Son,

Tucker

direct to Knoxville care of Genl H. Heth and I may probably get it, will write whenever I can get an opportunity, thought don't expect many as the chances are few.

Letter, Thursday, October 30th, 1862

Knoxville
October 30th, 1862

Dear Pa,

I am on a flying trip from Cumberland Gap with Dispatches, and have to be off again in half an hour.

I received the letter of Peyton's, Norman's and Ma's of the 10th one that Mr Rayl sent while in Ky was lost. I am with Col Ashby as aide while he is comdg the 3rd Cavalry Brigade.[13] We are ordered to Kingston from there to Middle Tennessee and expect to have an active campaign. I have money enough to last til we are paid off I think. We expect to be paid in a few days I don't spend much money because I can't find any thing to buy, can't find even a pair of Gloves in town are swept out.

All the troops have left the Gap except one Brigade, and the troops seem to be winding their way to-wards Nashville[14] I will write Peyton as soon as possible and whenever I can find time and place will write whenever I can My very best love to Ma Norman Uncle March and family and all relations and friends.

Better still direct to Mr Rayl care as I don't know where I will be.
Ever Your Devoted Son,
Tucker
I am in excellent health.
Tell Norman I have a very fine horse called "Rebel"
Ashby is a cousin of Turner Ashby, a Virginian (H. M. Ashby)

Colonel Henry M. Ashby, a cousin of Turner Ashby,
led a Confederate cavalry regiment in Henry Heth's brigade.
Library of Congress Prints and Photographs Division
https://hdl.loc.gov/loc.pnp/cwpb.06045

Letter, Thursday, November 6th, 1862

Knoxville
November 6th, 1862

Dear Pa,

Col Ashby and I came to this burg day before yesterday, to report for orders. Our command has gone to Kingston preparatory to a campaign in Middle Tenn presently our plan of operations is confidential. Genl McCown[15] wishes to place Ashby in command of all Cavalry, which is a great honor for so young a man (only 23) but has proved himself to be a good and dashing officer. I am acting as his <u>Adjutant</u> <u>General</u>, and if he is promoted to a Brigade as many think probable, I can be promoted to <u>Captain</u>. My present position is much more agreeable than with the old company.

I met Captain Maurice on the cars a few days ago, he promised to call and tell you I was well and then on my way to the Gap, with Dispatches.

There is great dissatisfaction in this Army with several Generals & Colonels have sent in their resignations and I heard one of our <u>Major Generals</u> say that if Smith provoked him much more he would leave. Bragg & Smith are cursed loud & deep by nearly the whole Army, and unless Johnson or Beauregard or some man in whom the men have <u>confidence</u> this army will never accomplish any-thing.

While Bragg was in full retreat after the battle of Perryville, Prentice in the *Louisville Journal* stated that <u>Buells</u> veteran army was cut to pieces, and that Buell was concentrating his raw levies preparing to fall back on Louisville, and said further that the Rebel Army may be expected in front of the city in a few days and there certainly was but <u>one</u> single Division cmdg by Clay Smith[16] that followed us to the Mountains, while Bragg was running and burning wagons &c besides demoralizing and breaking down his army and the policy pursued by Smith in Lexington was very partial. Genl Buford[17] whom he selected to recruit a Brigade of Kentuckians, was before we came into the State a strong <u>Union</u> man and had been to Washington to get a commission in the <u>Lincoln</u> Army,

Confederate Kentucky cavalryman John Hunt Morgan
led several daring raids that garnered great acclaim.
Library of Congress Prints and Photographs Division
https://lccn.loc.gov/2004662218

and hampered John H. Morgan in such a manner that he was prevented from raising a Division which he could have done with perfect ease, as it was he raised a Brigade in spite of Smith. Buford's command now is very much dissatisfied with him and a great many have deserted and gone back home, and they cannot be censured much because both Bragg & Smith repeatedly in public speeches assured the people that we would hold the state & cross the Ohio and carry the war into the enemies Country. But for Genl Smith, I candidly believe that Genl Heth could & would have taken Covington and Cincinnati as a matter of course must have been ours because the River was so low none of their Gun Boats could operate, and in Cincinnati was stored nearly the whole Winter Supplies in the way of clothing &c if Buell's Army enough to have supplied nearly our whole army. When as it is now they are almost naked & barefooted, and independent of all this Kentucky is lost to us forever, even were we to drive the Yankees out of the State the people would not believe we were going to stay, and they have good cause for it when one of our Full Generals tells them a lie.

I have drawn 2 months pay which will last me some time though everything is very high. Silk handkerchiefs 5 dollars a piece Whites 2 dollars, and everything in proportion, a Uniform is worth 150 dollars and scarcely anything to be had at that.

I hear of a letter directed to Lexington for me, will get it in a day or so, it is with General Heth's command. I hope Ma & all are well my very best love to her and all my relations & friends, not forgetting yourself.

Ever Your Devoted Son,
Tucker
I am as usual in excellent health.

Letter, Wednesday, November 12th, 1862

Knoxville
November 12th, 1862

Dear Ma,

I wrote Pa several days ago but have not received an answer so far. I hope it came safe to hand, there was a letter for "Peyton" enclosed.

As you see I am still in Knoxville killing time. We are waiting for Kirby Smith to give us orders there is also rather bad news for me. Genl John Pegram is to be assigned to Col Ashby Brigade which throws him back to his Regt and me back to the Company, which I am very sorry for, as my position in it is very disagreeable, in fact I don't wish to go back even if I were Captain as it is composed of a class of men I don't admire, and if I can get any other position, I will gladly accept it.

Is there an opening that you know of in or about Richmond. I believe I had rather fight in the Old Dominion than any place else, and particularly as there is such great dissatisfaction in this department. We have or ought to have enough of Cavalry officers to command our Cavalry, without assigning Infantry Colonels as Pegram was. I have not found out anything to do yet but hope to be able to find something before long. I am like a "bandy ball" knocked first one side then another, if I do get a good permanent position I will stick to it like "grim death to a dead nigger" as the boys say.

Every thing is so high that I shall have to borrow 50 dollars from Mr Rayl & I drew 200 dollars but as things are here it doesn't last long. My Jacket & Pants cost 97$ a decent shirt 20$ and so on.

Major Wash Morgan brother of John H. Morgan was killed a few days ago near Lexington.[18] There is nothing new that I know of I am very well and hope this will find you all the same.

My very best love to all relations & friends not forgetting Pa & yourself.

Ever Your Devoted Son,
Tucker

Letter, Friday, December 5th, 1862

Camp near Murfreesboro
December 5th, 1862

Dear Ma,

We arrived here yesterday and reported to Genl Pegram, who we found at Genl Morgan's Quarters, he told me he had seen you in Richmond, and that you were all well, which I was glad to hear as not hearing for some time I feared that some of you might be sick. We have a very large army here and if Genl Bragg will "let" them, will whip out this Yankee Army. Our cavalry bring in prisoners every day. Our lines extend to the River (Cumberland).

Now that Pegram has arrived I am thrown out of position, unless I return to the Company which is at Lavergne, 15 miles from Nashville, but don't be uneasy on my account, for I can look out for No. 1. I started in the Ranks and I can try it again. I don't know how to have letters directed as we are continuously moving, but if you direct to Genl Pegram's care, I may get them (at Murfreesboro).

Give me news from the Old Dominion when you write. Our news here is vary vague & uncertain hope this will find you all well, with much love to all.

I Remain Ever Your Devoted Son,

Tucker

Letter, Monday, December 8th, 1862

Head Qrts. 1st Ten Cav
near Murfreesboro
December 8th, 1862

Dear Pa,

I wrote you a day or two ago, but I drop another few lines to let you all know that John Morgan has made another brilliant dash, he took 13,000 fire arms 5 pieces of artillery and a large no of wagons &c near Hartsville, today.[19]

Our headQtrs are near Morgan's, the more I see of this man the more I like him he is simple and gentlemanly in his manners. We have had quite a fall of snow, and has not melted off yet.

Genl Pegram has taken command of the Brigade. I think the command will like him though they were very much prejudiced against him.[20] I have not made up my mind to return to my company or try to obtain some position here.

I wrote Ma to direct my letters to Genl Pegram's care, Murfreesboro. Hoping this will find you all well and with much love to all.

I Remain Ever Your Devoted Son,

Tucker

John Pegram put in a rather lackluster performance leading Confederate cavalry in the western theater before being sent east to command infantry. Library of Congress Prints and Photographs Division https://lccn.loc.gov/93513446

8

With John Pegram in the West
December 1862 to October 1863

Another gap in Tucker's correspondence appears between December 1862 and October 1863. Evidently, Tucker secured a position on new arrival John Pegram's staff and would remain there for the remainder of the war. We know little from Tucker about his activities, other than he rode a black horse, 14 1/2 hands high that was valued at $300.[1] Fortunately, we do have ample evidence of Pegram's activities and one of Tucker's fellow staff officers left a brief, but thorough, account of Tucker's time with Pegram in the West.

Confederate fortunes in the west soured dramatically after Tucker's letter in early December. In November, General Braxton Bragg had launched an offensive into Middle Tennessee, resolving to enter enemy territory and take up a favorable position and await attack. Ultimately, Bragg's Army of the Tennessee ended up near Murfreesboro, Tennessee. There it awaited the advance of Union general William S. Rosecrans' forces, who obligingly sortied forth from Nashville. The armies collided at Stones River on December 31, 1862. A bloody fight and bitter stalemate ensued, until January 2. A flanking movement by Confederate Maj. Gen.

John C. Breckinridge enjoyed initial success, but then suffered a disaster as it fell victim to massed Union artillery fire. John Pegram played a role in this defeat, as he had been ordered to cooperate with Breckinridge, but was out of contact on that fateful morning. Even Pegram's biographer noted that "Stones River was a miserable failure for John Pegram."[2] It was an inauspicious start to the New Year. After a poor performance there, Pegram would not do much better over the rest of 1863.

While the armies took time to lick their wounds after Stones River, the cavalry continued operations. On March 22, 1863, Pegram embarked on expedition into Kentucky "for the purpose of obtaining beef-cattle for the Confederate Army."[3] For several days, Pegram's cavalry moved about Kentucky, driving off Union resistance. Eventually, Union forces gathered and began to heavily press Pegram's men, which in turn forced Pegram "to resist the enemy" because "the safety of my command somewhat depended on giving the enemy a good check."[4] A short but sharp fight on March 29 stymied the Union troops, which allowed Pegram the chance to withdraw and get his men ready to cross the Cumberland River and put his men on the opposite side of a natural obstacle from his pursuers. As his men got the cattle across the Cumberland River the night of March 29, Pegram also prepared a defensive position outside of the town. Union forces probed Pegram's position during the night, before retiring. Tucker impressed Pegram during the night of March 29-30, prompting the general to note in his report that "by his personal efforts during the whole night he rendered such service as commanded the admiration of all who saw him."[5] Pegram's forces continued to operate in Kentucky until June, when he returned to Tennessee after suffering a defeat inflict by an inferior Union force.[6]

Pegram's lackluster cavalry career continued for the remainder of 1863. During the summer, Union Maj. Gen. William S. Rosecrans maneuvered Gen. Braxton Bragg's army out of Tennessee and pushed it south into Georgia. There, the two armies clashed at Chickamauga in September. During that campaign, Pegram provided poor information while scouting and generally failed to handle his brigade well. As one historian has noted, "John Pegram did not excel at any level during the campaign" and that "the quality of the information Pegram provided was not on par with the intelligence" that other provided.[7]

The most comprehensive account of Tucker's activities with Pegram in the West comes from fellow staff office Raleigh Travers Daniel, which was deposited with Tucker's papers at the Museum of the Confederacy.

A friend and fellow staff officer, Raleigh T. Daniel,
penned a lengthy account of Tucker Randolph after the Civil War.
Chamberlayne, *Ham Chamberlayne, Virginian*

R. T. Daniel's Account:
"Reminiscences of the military career of Tucker Randolph from Dec 31st
1862 until his death in the Second Battle of Cold Harbor June 1864"[8]

The day of the first engagement before the town of Murfreesboro, Tennessee Dec 31st 1862, I joined the Cavalry Brigade of Genl John Pegram, to whose command I had been recently appointed A.A.G. which was posted on the extreme right of the Confederate lines. Then & there I became first associated with Tucker Randolph acting as Volunteer Aide de Camp to Genl Pegram, who entertained a warm personal attachment for him, a high estimate of his soldierly qualities, and an earnest desire to find some permanent position for him befitting his merits. I think he found Randolph attached to Col Henry Ashby's 1st Tenn Cav Regt when he assumed command of the Brigade.

During the two days fighting on our left Genl Pegram made a bold reconnaissance in rear of the enemy's lines; and on his return to the front made a brilliant dash on a strongly guarded waggon train, which proved to be under close range of the enemy's main line of battle on Stone river. Eleven waggons loaded with bacon, coffee, sugar & other stores, together with 150 prisoners, were brought into our lines under a fearful fire of infantry and artillery. These comprised the services of the Brigade during the series of actions known as the battle of Murfreesboro, which concluded with the failure of Breckenridge's brilliant charge on Stone river, in the presence of Genl Pegram, who held his command in readiness to follow up the success that never came. Genl Bragg ordered this attack against the earnest protest in council of all his subordinate commanders.

Twelve hours later commenced the retreat towards Chatanooga, when this command was charged with the honorable & responsible position of rear guard of the army; which entailed upon it three consecutive days and nights of marching & skirmishing with the enemy's advance guard relieved only by snatches of sleep in the saddle or in fence corners, with no time to cook rations.

In the charge on the waggon train Randolph led the van saddle to saddle with his commander, and during the scenes referred to he was ever vigilant and intrepid, evincing discretion beyond his years.

Two weeks later the command was ordered to the vicinity of Knoxville, East-Tennessee, to form an integral [part] of the line of the defence extending Northward into Virginia, consisting of forces posted to defend the approaches through the gaps of the Cumberland & Alleghany ranges, one important object being the protection of the salt works at Saltville, Va, the chief dependence for that staple of both the armies & the citizens.

While here Genl Pegram was ordered to make a reconnaissance in force advancing across the Cumberland mountains toward the Kentucky river, into the "blue grass district," and to bring back all the cattle that might be collected on the route. Accordingly, at the head of 1700 horse and a field battery of 6 pieces, with only baggage or camp equipage, prepared for the greatest celerity of action, he started from Kingston in a Northwesterly direction passing through Morgan C.H. Jamestown, Pall Mall to the Kentucky line, there to Monticello crossing the Cumberland river to Somerset, Stanford, Danville to Hickman's Bridge on the Kentucky river, a distance of more than 200 miles. The distance from Morgan C.H. to Monticello, over a desolate mountain region, was crossed by marches of 40 miles a day. Here we struck the enemy 5000 strong, who, ignorant of the Confederate numbers, were pushed back with daily skirmishing to the Kentucky river, which was as far into the enemy's country as it was thoroughly advisable to penetrate, for all this section of the state was devoted to the Union cause.

As the Confederates retired the enemy were informed by their friends on the route of their actual numbers, whereupon they pushed them with great vigor, with frequent attempts to throw troops around on the flanks. Nevertheless, Genl Pegram had collected nearly 2000 head of cattle, which he was driving ahead of him, while he retarded the enemy's advance by frequent stands in line of battle, from which he skillfully withdrew at discretion. Reaching Somerset, with all the captures between him & the Cumberland river about 7 miles in his rear, it was found necessary to give battle in earnest. The situation was most perilous, requiring all his skill & coolness to save from surrender or destruction his small band by vastly superior numbers, with a broad river behind him. The battle of Somerset was long & bloody, but fought with such steadfastness by the Confederates that as darkness suspended the conflict they held their original positions on the field. During the whole conflict details of men were crossing the cattle in boats, which was wholly accomplished at midnight, and at break of day the last two of this gallant commanded landed on the South bank of the river -- they were Genl John Pegram & Tucker Randolph.

The Confederates held the river line without further molestation until the cattle were three days on the road to our lines, when they returned to the neighborhood of Knoxville (I have not thought it necessary to encumber this synopsis with details of sharp encounters at Dnaville, Standford, & other points on the route).

The Brigade remained in Camp, drilling & otherwise preparing for the approaching campaign until August 1863, when it was ordered to join the army of Tennessee near Chattanooga, and Genl Pegram was placed in command of a Cavalry Division, comprised of his own & Genl Davidson's[9] Brigade, with a portion of which he first met the enemy on the 10th. One the 12th he struck & held at bay two hours Wilder's Lighting Infantry Brigade, the pick troops of Crittenden's Corps.[10] On Saturday, Sept 19th Genl Pegram, with most of Davidson's and some of his own Brig, held the main advance of the enemy in check until our Infantry cld deploy and relieve him, to open the memorable battle of Chickamauga.

In all these scenes of action Tucker Randolph was at the side of his general, or executing his orders with that dash & discretion that distinguished him…[11]

R. T. Daniel

March 23rd 1887

On August 20, 1863, the Confederate War Department issued orders assigning Pegram to the Army of the Northern Virginia. Additional clarification came on October 11, when further orders specified that Pegram should report to Lieutenant General Richard S. Ewell, commanding the Second Corps of the Army of Northern Virginia. Pegram would receive the command of an infantry brigade composed of the 13th Virginia Infantry Regiment, 31st Virginia Infantry Regiment,

49th Virginia Infantry Regiment, 52nd Virginia Infantry Regiment, and 58th Virginia Infantry Regiment. Pegram's brigade was part of Major General Jubal A. Early's division.[12] As part of the Pegram's headquarters, Tucker Randolph would be returning to Virginia, too.

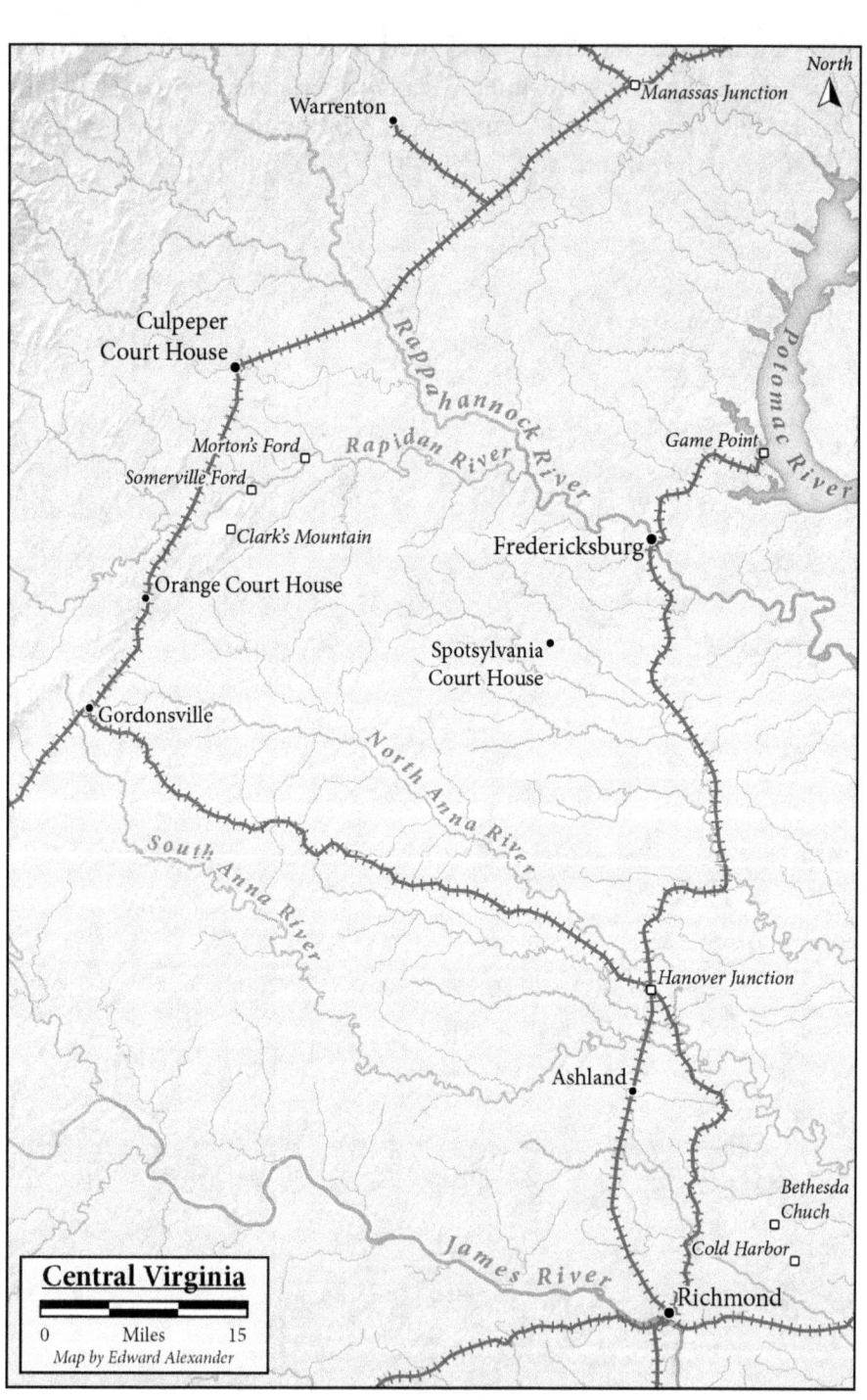

North

Warrenton

Manassas Junction

Culpeper
Court House

Morton's Ford

Somerville Ford

Rapidan River

Rappahannock River

Game Point

Potomac River

Clark's Mountain

Fredericksburg

Orange Court House

Spotsylvania
Court House

Gordonsville

North Anna River

South Anna River

Hanover Junction

Ashland

Bethesda
Chuch

Cold Harbor

James River

Richmond

Central Virginia

0   Miles   15

Map by Edward Alexander

9
With the Army of Northern Virginia
October 1863 to May 1864

When Tucker returned with Pegram to Virginia, he joined an army that had fought many hard battles and gained a great reputation. During his convalescence from his wounds and service with Pegram, Tucker had missed many of the great events in the East. When Tucker fell at Kernstown, Stonewall Jackson had just begun his meteoric rise; Lee had yet to take command of the major Confederate field army; and the Confederates faced the less than energetic Major General George B. McClellan. When Tucker returned, the situation had changed drastically. Jackson had fallen victim to friendly fire at the battle of Chancellorsville and died soon thereafter; Lee had led the Army of Northern Virginia into two unsuccessful invasions of the North in both the summer of 1862 and 1863; and Major General George G. Meade led the Army of the Potomac.

When Tucker went east, he found an army battered after its defeat at Gettysburg, but full of spirit and led by a still-aggressive Robert E. Lee.

Letter, Tuesday, October 20th, 1863

Head Qrs Pegram's Brigade
Early's Div, Ewell's Corps
Near Rapphannock Station
October 20th, 1863

My Dear Ma,

I received a letter from you that had been sent out west day before yesterday. We have been continually on the move since we left Richmond we arrived at Orange CH Sunday the 11th and found the army had left on the 10th,[1] the Genl procured a horse and went to Madison CH that night. I remained until Monday morning [12th], and then started with Norman who came in Sunday evening, for Culpeper C.H. which place we reached about 3 oc. We found some 300 prisoners there, which Stuart had captured.[2] We passed on and caught up with the Genl about 8 miles beyond, found him in command of his Brig, moving at a snails pace, which must disgusted us, coming from the cavalry where we were accustomed to move so rapidly. We camped that night about 10 o'c and moved on in the morning [13th] by day light for Warrenton Springs which place we found had been almost totally destroyed by the Yankees. We then moved on to Warrenton, Fauquier Co. a very pretty place, near which we massed our Div, nearly all of Ewell's Corps was near the place, and a beautiful sight it was, the country is completely desolate with some few exceptions, no fences and scarcely a living creature to be seen, the face of the country looks as desolate as you can imagine.

We moved to camp near Warrenton and left the next morning [14th] going in the direction of Manassas. We made a large detour to get on the flank of the enemy supposed to be in force, but found only some cavalry.[3] We then marched in the direction of Bristow Station, where Hill's corps preceded us, and when quite near that place heard fighting ahead, but before we came up all the Infantry fight was over. We had some heavy artillery fighting during a part of which the Gen'l sent Norman with Gen'l Early under quite a heavy fire of shell, but no one was hurt, the Infantry was of Heth's Div, 2 Brigades were sent in and soon whipped out with heavy loss. Why more were not sent in is unaccountable. Hill would not let Heth put in his whole division, which was very wrong, the Yankees threw a whole Corps against 2 Brigs.[4] We first drove them back and they seeing our small forces turned on them. We had 3 Genls wounded, Cook [Posey] & Kirkland, the enemy's loss we don't know.[5] We lost about 1500 prisoners and lost 5 pieces of artillery caused by a Brig of North Carolinians running before some Yankee skirmishers.[6] We tore up the railroad from Bristow Station to the Rappahannock. Our Brig worked during a hard rain in which we all were completely soaked. We were also welcomed by a hard rain during the night.

General Jubal A. Early led the division in which John Pegram's brigade served.
Library of Congress Prints and Photographs Division,
https://hdl.loc.gov/loc.pnp/ds.01484

The next day we did nothing but lie in camp. We moved next morning.

Our Brig bringing up the rear, we were not disturbed at all by the enemy. Yesterday morning just as we were moving out of camp there came up one of the most violent storms I ever saw my horse could scarcely get along against the wind, the rain came in our faces like shot. We were soon as wet as rats and very cold. When we got to the river, found we could not cross for 3 or 4 hours, so we went into camp, crossed over that evening, and are now on the South of the Rappahannock where will probably remain for several days.

Norman left this morning to tramp after our Chest &c.

All well, love to all.

Your Devoted Son,

Tucker

Tell Pa he had best buy some more of the cloth for Winter.

Letter, Wednesday, January 20th, 1864

Somerville Ford
January 20th, 1864

My Dear Ma,

I have been awaiting a letter from <u>somebody</u> for the last ten days, but receiving none I at last am compelled to write myself as no one will write me. Norman's is the only letter I have received from home since I came up. If you all knew how excessively dull it is here, you would certainly write often. Our daily routine is as follows, with some few variations. We get up about nine o.c. wash down to the waist (this is invariable) get breakfast, which we make as long as possible, then we adjourn to our tents, and Trav⁷ and myself take a smoke (this is also invariable), if we have any business which is seldom, we perform it, if not we read, if we have anything, taking several smokes in the mean time (this is very <u>mean</u> time). The Gen'l goes off to the Court Martial, when he returns about 4 o.c. we prepare for dinner, at which we usually remain until dark, adjourn to our tents and take a smoke (Trav & myself). We light a candle, either read or play cards until bedtime which varies according to the amount of amusement we can muster up, then we undress very deliberately, before the fire, blow out the candle, and roll under the blankets to think of things innumerable, until we fall asleep, and there is the end of one day of our existence, you can take the above for a fair example of our very interesting life here.

Yesterday the scene was varied by the execution of a deserter.

Trav and I rode over to the regiment of the condemned, had the grave dug, coffin set out, details made re, at 3 o'c the Gen'l formed the Brigade in three sides of a square. I then went after the prisoner, formed the procession by twos, ten men an officer in front, prisoner attended by two chaplains. We moved in at corner of square--then off to the grave. The Charges &c were read by Trav Daniel, then the prisoners and chaplains knelt and prayed, the Gen'l and staff dismounted and took off their hats. When the prayers were over, the prisoner was led round to his coffin blindfolded, and made to kneel, the command was given ready'aim'fire, and ten missiles of death were buried in his breast he started and fell back, the surgeons went up to him, and in a few seconds his soul had passed to its maker, his body was placed in the coffin, the command sent to their quarters, and the body buried. this man was shot for desertion, three times repeated, the day was intensely cold, and the wind blowing "big guns" we were nearly frozen when we got to camp. The prisoner was a member of the 49th Regt, a large man with a very bad face, you would be surprised to see with what perfect coolness men look on such a sight as this, in half an hour, after, they are just as merry as ever. We were having a game of chess within twenty minutes after those fatal shots were fired.

Please send up something to read by the first opportunity. We are completely out. I have jars and bottles packed to send down by the first chance I would like to have some thin socks also, these I have are too thick.

If you will send me a French Grammar and reader, Trav Daniel and myself will study French this is a very fine opportunity. My best love to all. Write soon.

Ever Your Devoted Son
Tucker

Letter, Thursday, January 21st, 1864

Somerville Ford
January 21st, 1864

My Dear Pa,

I wrote Ma a long letter yesterday, before hers of the 18th came to hand. I am very glad to hear Jack Tucker has arrived safe, tell him he must write me a long letter about his operations in the north.[8]

My letter to Norman which Ma says he would not show her was rather a severe criticism on his spelling. I think I might include Ma in that class sometimes, but it really is a shame for Norman to spell so badly, writing a bad hand is nothing in comparison to it. Norman is getting too old to spell so badly. I tried to impress it on him in my letter.

Our bill of fare at present is very good so Ma need have no apprehension on that score.

We are suffering more for something to amuse ourselves with, than any-thing else. We have read everything we could lay our hands on and are now entirely out.

Ambrose Ranson[9] went to Richmond yesterday. I don't know how long he will be able to stay. I suppose he will stay either at Mrs. Pegram's[10] or Mr. Daniel's.[11]

What is Norman doing now, and what are your plans with regard to him next spring. It is probably that the seat of war may again be transferred to the vicinity of Richmond in that case his present Battalion will be as good a place as he can find, if I see any chance for him will let you know. My affairs remain in the same position. The Gen'l expects to get a leave soon and will see what he can do.

My best love to all.

Ever Your Devoted Son

Tucker

Send some Paper and Envelopes

The letter of the "Joint Stock Company" came to hand last night will answer it to-day. Please tell me who "Virginia" is, who writes in the "Joint Stock" letter for I cannot imagine who it is, don't tell her, whoever she is that I made the inquiry for it would not be very complimentary to say the least.

Letter, Sunday, January 24th, 1864

Head Quarters Army No Va
January 22nd, 1864
General Order }
No 7}

The Commanding General considers it due to the Army to state that the temporary reduction of rations has been caused by circumstances beyond the control of those charge with its support.

Its welfare and comfort are the objects of his constant and earnest solicitude, and no effort has been spared to provide for its wants. It is hoped that the exertion now being made will render the necessity of short duration, but the history of the Army has shown that the country can require no sacrifice too great for its patriotic devotion.

Soldiers you tread with no unequal step the road by which your fathers marched through suffering, privation, and blood to independence. Continue to emulate in the future as you have in the past, their valor in arms, their patient endurance of hardships, their high resolve to be free, which no trial could shake, no bribe seduce, no danger appal, and be assured that the just God, who crowned their efforts with success will in his own good time send down His blessing upon yours.

R. E. Lee
General

Somerville Ford
January 24th, 1864

My Dear Ma,

I give you on the preceding page a copy of General Lee's order to the Army, it is a very eloquent and well timed address, so very modest and dignified, and speaks to the character of our noble leader.

I made a visit to Clarke's Mountain to-day, where we have a signal station, the day was most lovely like a spring day. We had a very fine view, could see large encampments of the enemy stretching towards the Rappahannock.

You must keep this order, put it in my desk. Tell me who is "Virginia" who wrote with Miss Rosalie and Eloise. I cannot for my life think who it is be sure not to let her know that I made the inquiry.

Love to all, no news.

Your Devoted Son,
Tucker

Send me some thin cotton socks by the first opportunity, these thick ones are exceedingly uncomfortable.

General Robert E. Lee led the Army of Northern Virginia.
Credit: Library of Congress Prints and Photographs Division,
https://lccn.loc.gov/2006677471

Letter, Thursday, January 28th, 1864

Somerville Ford
January 28th, 1864

My Dear Norman,
Your letter of the 23rd came to hand last night together with John Tucker's.[12]

It is singular that I do not get more of your letters. It may be that the stamps come off & they will not send them through the office.

I have paid Battle for the Halter.

Barney (for it is the name of the boy) seems to pay very good attention to Sallie, and she was improving, but the last day or two she has been rather under the weather but is better.

We have had for the last few days the most delightful weather that I ever experienced in January, it has been like Spring.

I hope by this you have received my replies to the young ladies letters. No news at all. Love to all.

Your Devoted Brother,
Tucker

Letter, Wednesday, February 3rd, 1864

Somerville Ford
February 3rd, 1864

My Dear Ma,
Yours of the 13th is to hand.

I saw Pa's advertisement about Fanny, hope you will be able to recover her. I think I can buy a horse up here for $600 and can send Sallie home she works very well either in single or double harness.

I strongly suspected it was Mrs. Duncan who wrote the letter and was very near writing to her direct but you said the letters were written by the "three girls" and as I did not suppose you would include Mrs. Duncan in that list, thought it could not be her, but I shall like to hear from her at all times, and will try to amend my unfortunate mistake.

The Grammar came all right many thanks for it I am nearly out of stationery, send me some nice paper and envelopes by the first chance.

I am going tomorrow to build quarters for the Brigade, as we have to move so as to be near the Div Commissary, the roads are getting bad it is blowing very cold, but will not last long.

Has not *Jean Valjean* been published yet, if there are any new novels out send them to us, we are much in need of something read.[13]

Love to all, all well.

Your Devoted Son,

Tucker

Letter, Tuesday, February 9th, 1864

Somerville Ford,

February 9th, 1864

My Dear Pa,

For the last three or four days we have been having some rather exciting times.

On the morning of the 6th, we were startled by Artillery firing over at Morton's Ford about four (4) miles below this place,[14] very soon orders came for us to move down to that point as rapidly as possible. We arrived there about 1 o'c, found the enemy on this side in some force.[15] We were placed in the trenches, throwing out skirmishers. We had some little firing among the skirmishers, and an occasional shot from the enemy's Artillery on the opposite side of the river.

A short time after sunset, our skirmishers advanced, the enemy giving back when a sharp fight commenced. We threw out two additional companies from each Regt, to support our skirmishers, the enemy held Dr Morton's house,[16] and for which we had to fight quite hard, the fighting continuous until it became so dark we could only see the flashes of the guns.

When we drove the enemy's advance back to the line of battle, we opened on them with Artillery, and must have caused considerable loss to them, as the shells were seen to explode in their ranks (This was the 1st Howitzers from Richmond).[17] The enemy threw shells on our works at the distance of two miles, wounding one officer of the battery slightly.

We had nearly the whole corps at the ford, our Div, Earlys, was in front of the ford, under the command of Col Evans of Gordon's Ga Brig,[18] Gen'l P had gone that morning to see some relations near Gordonsville, but returned on the morning of the 7th.

Georgian Clement A. Evans commanded Early's division, of which Pegram's brigade was a part, during the action at Morton's Ford. Library of Congress Prints and Photographs Division, https://www.loc.gov/item/2002710118

Our Brigade[19] and Gordon's did all the fighting (Ramseur's[20] N.C. did some skirmishing) I saw, and nearly all the dead were in our front, some few in Gordon's. Capt Randolph of the 49th Va was in command of the skirmishers of our Brig, and behaved very well.[21]

The enemy did not fight well, had to be forced up by their officers. We could hear them cursing this way very plainly, about midnight they re-crossed the river, leaving about 17 dead in our hands, carrying off all the wounded, the enemy had about one division on this side,[22] no artillery, or if they had any, they did not use it. Genl Handcock commanded, it was supposed the enemy had a corps in our front.[23]

Our loss was surprisingly small, only four men slightly wounded in our Brig, and one or two killed in the Div.[24] The enemy captured two

A drawing of the skirmish at Morton's Ford, as seen from the Union side.
The house on the right is that of Dr. Morton.
Alfred R. Waud, Scene at the late reconnaissance at Morton Ford - night.
United States, Virginia, Morton's Ford, 1864.
Library of Congress Prints and Photographs Division,
https://www.loc.gov/item/2004660319/

Lt's and about 30 men, at the ford when they crossed, belonging to the Stonewall Brig. We captured about 60 prisoners in all.

We remained in the works all day (the 7th) but did nothing, on the morning of the 8th all the Yankees had disappeared except a small picket, so we returned to camp. We had a very cold time, the hills we were on, were swept by the wind, which was very cold and piercing.

The enemy made a little demonstration at Barnets Ford, in Hill's front. No loss I believe.[25]

I received Norman's note. I hope he recovered the horse. All well, love to all.

Your Devoted Son,

Tucker

Please send me by Trav D. who will return in three or four days,

Some nice paper & envelopes

3 prs cotton socks (thin)

If you can send small box with good bread, peas, dried fruit or any thing of the kind it will be very acceptable for we are on short rations now.

Any new novels that may be out we have *Silas Marner*.[26]

Send me a pair of Woolen Gloves, these I have are worn out, my buck gloves are good also some good tobacco.

Letter, Saturday, February 13th, 1864

Somerville Ford
February 13th, 1864

My Dear Pa,

The books and letters reached me safely many thanks for them. I suppose before this Trav Daniel has given the letter and list of things I would like to have.

I have no intention of buying another horse for myself, but thought in the event Frannie could not be found that I would send my horse home, who works very well in harness and buy another for myself.

I think before the spring campaign is over (unless she is disabled in the meantime) I will have to send Sallie home and take the mare.

Smith arrived yesterday and told me he brought up a box, it is still at the C.H. but will try to send for it today.

When Smith left here for Richmond I halfway promised to buy a pair of shoes from him, he brought them up with him and as he is on his way to join Mosby he could not carry them, so although I did not need them had to taken them, he gave 85$ for them in Charleston, so that the result is I am short this month, will not be able to pay my dress uniform bill with the remainder of my pay, so please send by Trav Daniel 100$, also some solution of arsenic as I am not entirely free from this eruption.[27]

It is reported that part of the Yankee Army has moved back towards Chesnut Gap and Sperryville, the pickets in our front have been more than usually alert. The Gen'l's old regiment, the 2nd Regular Cavalry are picketing in our front, one of the Serg't told our men that the regt had turned out 25 Genl's of whom 17 came South, and all the gentlemen came South. They are nearly all foreigners.

All well.

Ever Your Devoted Son,

Tucker

Letter, Tuesday, February 23rd, 1864

Somerville Ford
February 23rd, 1864

My Dear Pa,

Col J. J. Morrison who now commands the Gen'l's old Brig in East Tennessee,[28] is in Richmond, he is a good friend of ours, and was kind to me out West. I am going to write him he will probably call to see you, please show him some attention while he remains in the city. He is staying at the Ballard House.[29]

I rode to Clarke's Mountain near our camp yesterday and had a very fine view of the Yankee Army. We saw a division of Cavalry on Review also a large body of Infantry. It was a very pretty sight. The weather is very fine.[30]

Everything is perfectly quiet up here. Please send me the money I wrote for as soon as you can. Love to all.

Your Devoted Son,

Tucker

I received the paper you sent last night.

Letter, Friday, March 11th, 1864

Somerville Ford

March 11th, 1864

My Dear Pa,

Your's & Norman's letters reached me this morning. I saw by the papers that the stable had been burnt (we get the papers regularly every-day) but did not write waiting for a letter, as you would give me the particulars. It is indeed a great misfortune, independent of the intrinsic value, it will be difficult to replace the horses & at any price. I intended to have brought the mare into the field this summer and let the one I have rest. She was nearly thorough-bred and would have made a fine brood mare. I am very glad "Mary" is safe, and poor old "Sport" it would have distressed Ma to death for him to have been burnt. What Insurance had you on the whole?

I hope Ma will soon be well, it is useless to cry over "spilt milk" I have ceased to be surprized at anything since the war commenced. We have escaped this far remarkably, and should be thankful for it. Have you any idea who the parties were, who fired the stable?

I am glad to hear Norman did such good service, my experience of raids is that they terrify more than they injure, if vigorously pursued and harassed, they will be always worked in the long run.

Dahlgren's plan was a most diabolical one, and justly deserved the fate it met. I hope the Government will punish the prisoners as their conduct merits.[31]

I wrote by the Gen'l whom I suppose you have seen before this, that is, if he can find the time from Miss Cary's agreeable society.[32]

We are glad to hear that prices are falling. It has become impossible for soldiers to live on their pay, at least those below the rank of General.

Our officers look exceedingly bright at present. The enemy have been repulsed at every point they have attacked along the extended lines of the country at least two thousand cavalry placed "hors de combat" certainly, for Kilpatrick's command will not be fit for service, until they receive fresh horses and the political arena crowded with candidates at the North.[33] We may expect something in our favor, from their division. Our armies are much fuller than they have been for some time...

[Remainder of the letter is lost]

Letter, Thursday, March 17th, 1864

Somerville Ford
March 17th, 1864

My Dear Pa,

Two nights ago some one stole my Saddle which was within six steps of the tent. I think there will be no chance of finding it, as the person who took it will soon dispose of it. The saddle is well known in the Brigade, and from that reason I do not think any one would keep it. Probably Norman can get me one of the Yankee saddles that were captured the other day from Dahlgren's party. I prefer a "McClellan tree" Norman knows the character of it. That is decidedly the best saddle in the service. If you can get one send it by the General who will be coming up soon. Tis said, Misfortunes never come single, it seems to be the case with us at present. It seems to me you had better not buy any new horses until the currency becomes more settled when they will be cheaper.

I hope Ma has received entirely from her fright. I suppose she was very much alarmed about the raiders.[34] My best love to all.

Your Devoted Son,
Tucker

10
Spotsylvania Courthouse and the Mule Shoe
May 1864

Spring 1864 brought a change to the war in Virginia. On March 10, Ulysses S. Grant was appointed lieutenant general and received command of all the Union armies. Grant, however, made his headquarters with the most important of those armies, the Army of the Potomac. The spring campaign began on May 4, when the Army of the Potomac crossed the Rapidan River. Grant aimed to make Lee fight or get past his right flank. Pegram's brigade engaged in the battle at Wilderness on 5 May, but the general was hit in the leg. Seriously wounded, Pegram left the front, with Tucker accompanying him. Tucker remained away from the army until 10 May. Rejoining the brigade, he found the armies entrenched around Spotsylvania Courthouse. A segment of Lee's line formed a salient, vulnerable to attack, that became known as the "Mule Shoe." Union troops had launched a small-scale attack on the area on 10 May. Lee, seeing the danger of the advanced position, ordered a new line laid and the Mule Shoe evacuated. Before the Confederates could pull back, however, a massive Union attack on 12 May shattered the Confederate position, leading to fierce fighting at the "Bloody Angle" of

the Mule Shoe. Tucker's first letter of 16 May gives a hurried account
of Spotsylvania, while his letter of May 23 gives a longer account of the
entire Overland Campaign.[1]

Letter, Monday, May 16th, 1864

Hd Qrs Pegram's Brig
About 3 Miles from
Spottsylvania CH.
May 16th, 1864

My Dearest Ma,

I reached Orange CH. after a very disagreeable ride, on the morning
of the 10th inst and started for the command after a very tiresome ride
of about 40 miles reached it near the place on the morning of the 10th[2],
found the command in the trenches, the enemy shelling heavily the next
morning we moved in the trenches to another part of the line, but were
not heavily engaged, every attack of the enemy was repulsed with heavy
loss to them.[3] On the morning of the 12th the enemy carried the works
in front of Jones' Brig, Johnson's Div, capturing a large number of the Div.
and some pieces of Artillery, our men seem to have behaved very badly
immediately upon breaking our lines, a sense of a confusion ensued. Our
Brig was ordered out rapidly, and formed under the fire of the enemy.
Gen'l Lee exposing himself very much riding out in front of the Brig
with his hat off Gen'l Gordon told him we were Virginians, and led
him off.[4] We then gave three cheers and moved forward rapidly against
the heavy masses of the enemy. One Division charged them and drove
them before us inflicting heavy loss upon them, and retook the works
which the enemy had taken from Johnson's Div, holding them until the
next morning though exposed to a enfilading & cross fire of musketry &
artillery. We lost heavily in officers and men. Gen'l Lee complimented
the Brig and so did everybody. it was decidedly the most desperate charge
that has been made during the fight. We were supported by Gordon's
Brig and they deserve some credit for their work. Gordon has been made
a Major Gen'l.

Our Brig had when we left camp about 1300 men. We now have only about 850, and very few staffers. I am sorry to say that one of our Regts did not do very well, it was flanked on the left and lost its colors and some prisoners we captured one stand of colors. Our loss in officers has been very large, one regt the 52nd lost 2 killed and 10 wounded.

The enemy has [three words illegible] our front since the 12th inst we have been strengthening our works which are now almost impregnable with our Div behind them. the enemy has been very quiet for the last day or two and are supposed to be fortifying. What he intends doing we are at a loss to know, but suppose Gen'l Lee does. Trav Daniel is a little unwell, and at the Hospital. Ranson & I are the only staff officers with the Brig. Wilson is sick.[5] I have gotten the box, many thanks for it. My best love to all, will write again soon.

Your Dearest Son,
Tucker

General John B. Gordon led General Robert E. Lee to the rear after the collapse of the muleshoe salient at Spotsylvania.
Brady National Photographic Art Gallery Collection, Library of Congress, Library of Congress Prints and Photographs Division,
https://www.loc.gov/item/mss4429700229

Letter, Monday, May 23rd, 1864

Hd Qrs Pegram's Brig
Near Hanover Junction
May 23rd, 1864

My Dear Ma,

I saw Mr Purcell yesterday at the Junction and he told me you were in town. I wrote a short note yesterday to let you all know I was well. We are at a loss to know what the enemy are up to at present but Gen'l Lee is in glorious spirits we saw him yesterday So we think all is going on right. Such is the advantage of having confidence in the commander of the Army.

I will give you some account of our operations in the last two weeks. On Friday the 6th (the morning after I left with the General)[6] the enemy attacked our brigade about 9 o'c in not less than three lines by brigade front which we repulsed after about two hours of hard fighting our men reserved their fire until the enemy came within sixty paces then fired by ranks, the enemies loss was very heavy and ours very slight. Lt Col Goodman of the 13th[7] was slightly wounded but has reported for duty since nothing but skirmishing occurred during the day along the line but about Sun down Gen'l Gordon with his brigade moved upon the enemies right flank and rear. When he had passed along the extent of our front sweeping every thing before him, our brigade was ordered to wheel to the right and form perpendicular to the former line before the wheel was completed while Col Hoffman was endeavoring to bring round the left Gen'l Early caused the right wing to be moved forward along the front of the works it moved in this direction the left not having completed its wheel and endeavoring to get up with the right and center, until in front of the Stonewall brigade it encountered the enemies breast-works on a ridge nearly perpendicular to our fortified line (made of rotten logs). having no skirmishers out being surprised and the officers of the brigade having no information whatever of what was to be done or encountered the line never having completely formed It was somewhat staggered and confusion ensued (This was all the result of bad management not the conduct of the men). The line was however rapidly formed at the front of the ridge mentioned while the enemy panic-stricken fled from their works dark came on, and the movement ceased. If the movement had been commenced by Gordon half an hour earlier, and the officers of his brigade had been apprized of what was to be done, and given time to form the command for the purpose (the commanding officer was probably also a little slow), so as to give Gordon efficient support which all were ready and eager to do. Our men were never in better spirits or condition. The movement would have been one of the most hard, successful, and effective of the war, as it was second to but few this brigade cannot claim a share of it, which it should have had.

The next morning (7th) the brigade moved forward the right along the line of works to the enemies works, already mentioned in the ridge which were modified and connected with our works We remanned these during the day. There was some fighting in Longstreet & Hill fronts[8] but we do not know the particulars. Saturday night the Army commenced the movement to the right, and was I in motion all night but moved a very short distance. Sunday morning it was discovered that the enemy had disappeared from our front on that day the Army moved to nearby to present position (17th). We spent all Monday throwing up works.

Tuesday we were in reserve and moved from the right to the left of the Corps and back several times to support different parts of the line being very much exposed and fatigued. I joined the command this evening after a very hard ride from Orange CH. of about 40 miles having to make a detour with part of Rosser's Cavalry[9] to avoid the enemy who were between me and the Army, and found the command in rear of Fields Div,[10] the enemy pressing him quite heavily but were repulsed with heavy loss we moved over to the center in rear of Johnson's Div[11] and debouched about 1 o'c.

Wednesday the 11th we moved in the trenches on the left of Johnson's Div. but were soon relieved by Hay's brigade,[12] and retired to our former position in reserve. It commenced raining very soon after we left the front line, and rained nearly all day that night it was reported the enemy had retired from our front.

On the morning of the 12th Col Hoffman comdg brig was informed about an hour before day that Gen'l Johnson was expecting an attack on his line, which formed an angular semi-circle considerably well advanced beyond the general line. Our brigade was immediately formed in rear of Hay's brigade, the left of Johnson's making a double line. Just as we were placed in this position about day-light, the enemy advanced upon Johnson in several lines probably three or four, at least brigade front and carried the works capturing most of the Division about two (2) thousand men with but apparently slight resistance and very little firing, not with standing the warning which reached us through Gen'l Johnson and the other Gen'l so long before the attack was made, the whole conduct of the troops Artillery and Infantry would indicate surprise the artillery was neither in position nor condition to do any execution and was all captured firing I think only one shot (why our brig was not placed to support Jones or Staffords brgs[13] which were the points attacked instead of putting us in rear of Hay's I cannot imagine. We lost about twenty pieces of artillery and gave the enemy much encouragement for up to that time, we had repulsed them at every point with heavy loss and very slight to ourselves). Our brigade was immediately moved by the right flank rapidly in order to take the enemy in the works in their left flank and rear. We had moved but a very short distance when we encountered the enemy in the woods finding that we had not sufficiently changed our direction we threw our right further round, moved by the right flank to the rear of the enemies left and formed a line of battle at once, with a part of Gordon's brigade under the immediate supervision of Gen'l Lee (and Gordon) who by his manner and word indicated that the fate of the corps, perhaps the army, depended upon our conduct. The General rode out in front, raised his hat the boy cheered Gen'l Gordon led Gen'l Lee to the rear. We advanced forward with promptness, order, and impetuosity, sweeping before us very heavy masses of the enemy composed of several division principally Hancock's Corps driving them without pause and following them some distance beyond the outer line of works and maintaining our position beyond the right of the brig until an order from Gen'l Ewell we felt constrained to fall back to the works The enemy were massed and fleeing before us, so that almost every shot was effective and notwithstanding the rapidity of our advance, we killed and wounded a great many some of our boys used the bayonet this brig re-took that part of the works and occasionally feebly assaulted by the enemy who were easily repulsed. We held the position during the day though our left flank was very much exposed. That part of the line which this brig re-took was the greater portion and right of the line that had been lost a part of that line on our left was not weaker but was held by the enemy during the day there was also an interval of several hundred yards on our right unprotected.

Owing to the suddenness of our movement the formation on the left was not complete when we advanced upon the enemy and the ground was densely wooded and marshy owing to this and probably some other causes, but a small portion of the 58th our left regt came up with the rest of the brig and that portion was suddenly cut off and captured by a small body of the enemy which fled precipitously upon the fire of the left flank of the 13th Va., unfortunately taking the colors of the 58th Va with them about sixty or seventy of the men. The higher officers becoming satisfied that that part of the line which had been lost had been very injudiciously chosen, about 2 o'c on the morning of the 13th inst, we were withdrawn and a new line formed and fortified cutting off the bend which has been alluded to, which line we still occupy on 19th, though we brought the captured guns by hand and deposited them some distance in the rear in order that proper authorities might save them, they failed to do so, and during the next night they were quietly taken from a short distance in front of our line of skirmishers by the enemy. From the 13th to the 18th we had skirmishing along our front and some heavy artillery firing but no heavy attack on the part of the enemy we remaining entirely on the defensive (we speak of our corps).

On the 18th early in the morning the enemy with great apparent preparation advanced upon Gordon's & this brigade, driving in the skirmishers, but were checked by the latter and the Artillery and afterwards driven back to their former position with very considerable loss. The prisoners report that they advanced in two lines brigade and were much damaged by our Artillery.

The morning of the 19th the enemy disappeared from the front of this division and Rhodes which is the left of the Army. Our loss from the 5th to the 19th has been nearly one third (1/3) of the brigade mostly killed

& wounded Col Skinner was badly wounded in the head & will probably lose both eyes[14] Lt Col Kasey[15] Major Cooper[16] & many very valuable company officers killed & wounded the proportion of officers being very large. The spirits and morale of the brig is almost unconquerable, they think themselves equal to any number of Yankees that can be brought against them it is to be regretted that they cannot have that confidence in some portions of the other troops that is so desirable they have on their right Gordon's brig which merits and has their fullest confidence.

On the 19th the Corps moved round to the enemies right flank and rear and struck the enemies wagons but not a large force of the enemy, and our advance was checked and had to fall back. Our brig was formed and charged across a large open field driving the enemies two lines back and holding our position against a heavy force of the enemy until about 11 o'c at night when we were withdrawn and returned to our former position in the trenches. Our brig was very highly complimented by every one. Gen'l Ewell had his horse shot Major Lilly of the 52nd was wounded.[17] Our loss was about one hundred the next morning the 20th, we began to move to this place finding Grant was moving in this direction.

May 25th The enemy are in force on this side of the North Anna we are well entrenched and have a ford position and are ready for Grant whenever he comes Our force has been much increased by new arrivals and are stronger now than when we left the Rapid Ann. Gen'l Lee told one of our Surgeons that there was no such fighting on record as that done by this brigade and the he was proud of us!! This is a great deal for Genl Lee to say. Our boys are in fine spirits and feel confident of giving the Yankees a sound thrashing we are all in fighting.

We have been moved about so much and kept under arms so long that we feel like we would rather fight than not.

My best love to all at home some of you must write Send me a pair of pants by the first chance as the seat of these is becoming alarmingly thin.

How and where is Norman?

Your Devoted Son,

Tucker

(keep this letter)

An 1887 lithograph of the Union attack on the Bloody Angle.
The artist shows the close-quarters fighting and the intensity of the battle.
Library of Congress Prints and Photographs Division,
https://lccn.loc.gov/90712278

11
Death at Bethesda Church
May 1864

Tucker's letter of May 23 would be his last, as he would fall victim during the intense fighting of the Overland Campaign. While Pegram's brigade had been held in reserve at Spotsylvania — thereby giving Tucker such a great vantage point for his account of the action — that luck would not hold.

The end came at Bethesda Church. Grant, unlike Union generals before him, continued to put pressure on Lee's army. The Army of the Potomac drew nearer to Richmond, and by May 30, Lee and Grant faced each other on almost the same ground as the 1862 Battle of Gaines's Mill. On the evening of May 30, General Jubal A. Early moved toward Bethesda Church, and coming across an enemy force, drove them back. Later in the day, Early ordered the brigades of Stephen Dodson Ramseur and John Pegram (commanded by Georgian Col. Edward Willis) to attack.

Though both brigades were to have made the attack, only Pegram's stepped off. The men advanced across "a level, open field, one-half mile across…behind which artillery was massed…and bayonets bristling thick as leaves." Pegram's men marched on alone, their ranks the lone target of Federal fire. One Confederate recalled that "the enemy opened with the heaviest and most murderous fire I had ever seen with grape, canister, and musketry." With exposed flanks, fire came from all directions. According to one witness, the Confederate "line melted away as if by magic--every brigade, staff, and field officer was cut down (mostly killed outright) in an incredibly short time."[1] One of those who fell was Tucker Randolph, and fellow staff officer Frank Ranson wrote Joseph W. and Honoria Randolph to let them know of the death of their son.

> Hd Qrs Pegrams Brig
> May 31st 1864
>
> My Dear Sir,
> The painful & distressing duty devolves upon me to communicate to you, the death of your beloved son Tucker, who fell in a desperate charge made by our brigade on the evening of the 30th of May.
> I unfortunately was not near him when he fell, having been sent by Col Willis our Brigade Commander to another Part of the field.[2] The particulars of his death to his official family I am sorry to say I am not able to give. I have learned however that he was killed instantly and fell in the hands of the enemy. His fate is deeply lamented by the Comd & the Officers of the brigade. As his brother Staff Officer please accept my deep and heartful sympathy in behalf of his afflicted and beloved family. He needs no eulogy at my hand, his many virtues and exemplary life reminds us that "death loves a shining mark."
> I am my Dear Sir,
> Yours truly & sincerely,
> Frank Ranson[3]

Tucker's loss was deeply felt. One Richmond paper offered the eulogy that "Lieut. Randolph was one of the most promising young officers in our service. His gallantry was conspicuous…it may with truth be said that Virginia has offered no nobler sacrifice to this war than this youthful and brave officer." Tucker was buried on June 8, at Richmond's Shockoe Cemetery after a procession from St. Peter's Catholic Church.[4]

We know little about Tucker's immediate family after the war. Tucker's brother Norman continued to serve with John Mosby's command. He later went on to become a businessman and leader with the Confederate veteran community in Richmond. Tucker's father suffered the loss of his bookstore, which burned with all of its stock during the evacuation of Richmond in 1865. But, Joseph rebuilt and continued selling books in Richmond after the war. As with many other families, they had suffered from the war, lost one of their own, and carried on as best they could.

Tucker's military family suffered further loss as well. John Pegram recovered from his wound at the Wilderness and served with the Army of Northern Virginia nearly to the end. Shortly after marrying Hetty Cary, Pegram was killed at the battle of Hatcher's Run in early 1865.

Another military acquaintance, John Worsham, survived the war and went on to pen what would become a classic account of life as a Confederate soldier.

12

John Worsham's Account of Tucker Randolph

After the war, John Worsham (later author of the classic Confederate account, *One of Jackson's Foot Cavalry*), wrote an account of Tucker's days in F Company and the 21st Virginia Infantry.

Richmond Va. Mch 25. 1901

When I joined F. Company about the 1st of Apr. 1861, amongst the boys was one who was tall, and thin, with black hair and dark eyes, very youthful but with a determination of countenance that made him at times look much older than he was. His attention to duties and his aptness in learning new things in military matters attracted my attention. I became very much interested in him and soon J Tucker Randolph and myself became great friends. We later became mess mates and in that way more closely attached.

He was with the Company when it was ordered on Apr 21, 1861 to march to Wilton on the James River a few miles below Richmond, in what is known as the "Pawnee War," and was one of the few detailed that Sunday night for duty along the river, (we considered that a distinction

John Worsham, a member of F Company, was friends with Tucker.
When Tucker was injured at the Battle of Kernstown, Worsham helped get him to
safety. This photo shows Worsham in 1865, after years of hard service and injuries.
Worsham, *One of Jackson's Foot Cavalry*

amongst the 100 and more men present), as only about six were put on duty, Capt Cary of F. Company choosing them himself for that service. Thus at the tape of the first drum commenced the war record of that boy of 17.

He was with the company when ordered to Fredericksburg a few days later, also with it at Aquia Creek, and made himself as prominent by attention to duty that he was on June 5, 1861 made a Corporal. Being the tallest of the non-commissioned officers, he was placed on the right of the company, and on all occasions when the company was ordered to fall in, Tucker Randolph's tall form was there for the men to line up on. On the march the first man you saw was this boy marching at the head of his company, and when we joined the regiment our company being the right one he thus became the front man of the regiment.

F. Company was ordered to Richmond on June 14, 1861 to join the 21st Regiment of Va Infantry and while there he was with F. Company mustered into the service of the Confederate States Army, June 28, 1861, to date from Apr 21, 1861.

The regiment left for the North-West of Virginia (now known as West Virginia) on July 18, 1861. Soon after getting in the mountains more than half the men became prostrated by sickness, this doubled the duty of those who were well. Corporal Randolph was one of the few who retained his health, and many times when he would return to comp now on Middle Mountain, from Picket duty, which was ten miles in our front, he would be immediately detailed to cook rations and go back. He would go about this cheerfully, collect his men, put on accoutrements, shoulder arms and march away as if he had been in camp a week.

He had now been made a Sergeant and was with us in our Winter campaign with Jackson, a campaign that tried mens souls - body too. Uncomplainingly he endured those hardships. In our skirmish 3rd January he was one of the few who was cool and collected. After this skirmish Jackson finds that the enemy are in force and strongly fortified at Cumberland on the other side of the Potomac river and decides to cross and attack them in their stronghold. On the morning of Jany 5, 1862, he sent an order for F. Company to come to the front and lead the crossing of the river and attack on the fortifications. Tucker hailed this with joy, and as soon as the company was formed he stepped off as if he was on a frolic, he was one of the leaders in the song, the Pirates Glee, we were singing when we overtook Jackson and were singing at that time, the chorus "we will nail the black flag to the mast." Old Jack took off his cap to us and smiled all over, you could see him say to himself, "good, good."

My recollection is that it was Tucker and myself who went to the Hotel in Romney the morning after reaching there, to get a good meal once more. We found delicious buckwheat cakes, maple syrup & fresh butter on the table, to these we immediately paid our respects, they soon disappeared. A nice young lady waited on the table, she brought more, they were soon disposed of, and more, and more came, only to share the same fate. Finally, they stopped; we called for the young lady and politely asked if we could get a few more of those delicious cakes. She disappeared, but soon returned with the information, they were all gone. There were some nice rolls on the table and we thought we would fill up on those, and asked her for more syrup & butter, she politely told us they were out too. We left the Hotel in disgust--they could not give two boys a "square meal."

The Battle of Bethesda Church, as seen from Union lines, in this drawing by Edwin Forbes. Tucker Randolph was mortally wounded attempting to take this position. Forbes accurately notes along the bottom of the sketch that "the rebs charged form the woods, across the open, they could not advance beyond the fence. Their loss was very heavy."
Library of Congress Prints and Photographs Division,
https://lccn.loc.gov/2004661433

On leaving Romney and getting to Winchester we were kept very busy as a large force of Yanks were at Hagerstown with the seeming intention of descending on us at any time, and when they finally came in such force that Jackson thought best to retreat. Tucker was one of those who complained of leaving without a fight, but when we marched back from Mt. Jackson a few weeks later to Kernstown and there met Shields he was all enthusiasm. During that battle, the 1st Va. Regt. fought large odds, some lying down, fighting in one direction, some standing behind trees fighting in another direction. F. Company on the right behind a fence were fighting a force on our right in a field, some of them lying behind a fence, some standing up, some standing on the fence. Tucker was one of those standing on the fence and was loading and firing so cooly as if on drill, when he was shot in the hip and had to be carried from the field. He was taken back to Middletown that night, and there I found him next morning as we marched through on our retreat, and was fortunate enough to get him away by a close shave as our cavalry were leaving the town at one end and the yanks entering at the other.

The company lost a valuable soldier in Tucker Randolph, he was always ready for any duty and did it cheerfully, his soldierly qualities and readiness to help at all times made every man with whom he came in contact his friend. I think while he was absent wounded if he had signified his intention of returning to the company, when we reorganized in Apr 1862 he would unanimously have been elected a Lieutenant of the company. On his recovery he was made a Lieutenant and Aid to Brig Genl Jno. W. Pegram who at that time was in Kentucky. He joined Pegram and served there with him and accompanied Pegram to Virginia. There Pegram was put in command of a Brigade in Early's Division, Second Corps, Army Northern Virginia. We saw him a few days after he joined our army, on one of our marches we came across him sitting on his horse beside the road, as we pass the company and the regiment too gave him a reception of which I know he must have been proud. We saw him occasionally after that and he always met with the same warm reception. He had plenty of fighting at this time. In the Spring of 1864, he was at Wilderness, Spottsylvania C.H. & Hanover Junction. Everytime we hear of him it is something good, and we are proud of him. He has thus far gone through that bloody campaign without a scratch. We are now to meet Grant again. On the evening of May 30. 1864, Gen Early who now commands the Second Corps had orders to make a demonstration at Bethesda Church. His old Division was to make the attack, our division (Gordons) was to support it. We march pass the Church, turn to the left, cross a small branch, form line of battle in front of that stream and slowly follow the attacking force, until we were halted a told to lie down. It was here that we heard that Tucker Randolph had been killed in a charge with Pegram's Brigade. Thus died this brilliant soldier boy, just as all soldiers wish to die - at the front, in the thickest of the fight.

Another soul "passed over the river" to "meet under the shade of the trees," with the gallant spirits of his old mess mates William Exall, John Powell, Ned Rawlings & Bob Ellett they are gathered around their immortal leader "Stonewall Jackson."

John H. Worsham late of F. Company
21st Va Regt of Infantry
Second Brigade
Jacksons Old Division
Second Corps

Notes

Introduction

1. Jonathan Daniels, *The Randolphs of Virginia* (Garden City, New York: Doubleday, 1972), 18-24. See also: "Memoir of the Randolph Family," J.W. Randolph Papers, Virginia Historical Society, Richmond. Though unsigned, this manuscript is in the hand of Joseph Williamson Randolph, who was the family historian.

2. Bible Records in the Randolph Family Bible, formerly in the possession of Mrs. David T. Ayers (Janet Randolph Turpin Ayers) of Richmond, Virginia; a photocopy of these is in the J. W. Randolph Papers, Virginia Historical Society.

3. G. Brown Goode, *Virginia Cousins: A Study of the Ancestry and Posterity of John Goode of Whitby, a Virginia Colonist of the Seventeenth Century, with Notes Upon Related Families, a Key to Southern Genealogy, and a History of the English Surname Gode, Goad, Goode or Good from 1148 to 1887* (Richmond, VA: J. W. Randolph & English, 1887), 212.

4. Evelyn D. Ward, *The Children of Bladensfield* (New York: Viking Press, 1978), 101.

5. Goode, *Virginia Cousins*, 354-355.

6. Bible Records in the Randolph Family Bible.

7. Biographical sketches of Captain Tucker St. Joseph Randolph and Norman Vincent Randolph, Samuel Bassett French Papers, Library of Virginia.

8. Bishop John McGill to Tucker Randolph, MC-3 R-137 File, formerly at the Eleanor S. Brockenbrough Library, Museum of the Confederacy; and Ward, *Children of Bladensfield*, 101.

9. Eugene W. Ferslew, *Second Annual Directory for the City of Richmond to Which is Added a Business Directory for 1860* (Richmond: Eugene W. Ferslew, 1860), 204; Robert F. Strohm, *"J. W. Randolph, Bookman Extraordinaire," An Occasional Bulletin* of the Virginia History Society, No. 42 (June 1981): 7-8; and *The Diary of Edmund Ruffin: Volume 1: Toward Independence, October 1856-April 1861*, edited by William Kauffman Scarborough (Baton Rouge: Louisiana State University Press, 1972), 266, 473.

10. Henrico County Tax Records, 1859 and 1860, Library of Virginia; 1860 Census Slave Schedules, Microfilm, Library of Virginia; Ervin L. Jordan, Jr., *Black Confederates and Afro-Yankees in Civil War Virginia* (Charlottesville: University Press of Virginia, 1995), 11; and Gregg D. Kimball, *American City, Southern Place: A Cultural History of Antebellum Richmond* (Athens: University of Georgia Press, 2000), 11-27.

11. John Worsham, *One of Jackson's Foot Cavalry*, ed. James I. Robertson, Jr. (reprint; Jackson, TN: McCowat-Mercer Press, 1964 [1912]), 1-2.

Chapter 1

1. Most young Virginians supported secession enthusiastically, and like Tucker, joined militia organizations. As Peter S. Carmichael has noted, Civil War offered young white male Virginians the opportunity to demonstrate their manhood and honor, as well as fulfill political goals, such as returning Virginia to a position of leadership in the nation. Many of them thought that the political reorganization following secession would remove many "old fogies" from power, allowing the perceived decline of Virginia to be reversed. Peter S. Carmichael, *The Last Generation: Young Virginians in Peace, War, and Reunion* (Chapel Hill: University of North Carolina Press, 2005), 121-147.

2. Fort Sumter.

3. Commissioners William Ballard Preston, Alexander Hugh Holmes Stuart, and George Wythe Randolph had gone to Washington to consult with President Abraham Lincoln. The *Richmond Daily Dispatch* reported that the three men "were appointed Commissioners by the State Convention to visit Lincoln and ascertain his intentions towards the seceded States." The trio met with Lincoln on April 12 and 13 regarding his intentions towards the Confederate investment of Fort Sumter in South Carolina and Fort Pickens in Florida. The *Richmond Daily Dispatch* reported the result of the conference: Lincoln's "reply leaves no doubt of his intentions to attempt the subjugation of all the States who may oppose his Government. Preston, Stuart, and Randolph were reportedly "said to be disgusted with the arrogance of the Babboon of Illinois." *Richmond Daily Dispatch*, Monday, April 15, 1861 (Page 1, Column 4, "Local Matters").

4. The James River.

5. Charles Dimmock, a West Point graduate, served as a captain of the Richmond Gray and the Public Guard. Louis H. Manarin and Lee A. Wallace, Jr., *Richmond Volunteers: The Volunteer Companies of the City*

of Richmond and Henrico County, Virginia 1861–1865 (Richmond: Westover Press, 1969), 248-49.

6. Confederate forces under the command of P. G. T. Beauregard opened fire on Fort Sumter, thereby forcing its surrender and prompting United States president Abraham Lincoln to call for 75,000 volunteer troops. This call, in turn, led many states of the Upper South to secede. Daniel W. Crofts, *Reluctant Confederates: Upper South Unionists in the Secession Crisis* (Chapel Hill: University of North Carolina Press, 1989), 308-323.

7. John Moncure Daniel, the secessionist editor of the *Richmond Examiner*. Daniel had written a sharp editorial that cast various figures as animals. Abraham Lincoln appeared as "an ugly and ferocious Orang-Outang," who ruled a menagerie of Virginia politicians who Daniel thought impeded Virginia's secession. One of these politicians, Marmaduke Johnson, objected to the mockery--he appeared as a fat horse who "neighed submission." Upon encountering Daniel in the street, Johnson assaulted Daniel. Richmond's mayor, Joseph Mayo, quickly intervened and demanded a peace bond from both men, which defused the chances of a duel. Peter Bridges, *Pen of Fire: John Moncure Daniel* (Kent, OH: Kent State University Press, 2002), 168-169.

8. The Union garrison at Fort Sumter surrendered on April 13 and formally capitulated on April 14.

9. The Richmond Fayette Artillery, a militia unit, had been formed in 1821 and named in honor of Marquis de LaFayette. Manarin and Wallace, *Richmond Volunteers*, 89.

10. John Letcher.

11. According to the *Richmond Daily Dispatch*, "patriotic and soul-stirring addresses [were] delivered by Messrs J. B. Sheffey, W. M. Ambler, C. Irving, Jno. M. Patton, Jr.., G. L. Gordon, and B. R. Welford, Jr. The reception accorded to the speakers was but an echo of that sentiment

of loyalty to section, with is the distinguishing characteristic of the true Southron." *Richmond Daily Dispatch*, Monday, April 15, 1861 (Page 1, Column 4, "Local Matters").

12. Wyatt M. Elliott, a graduate of the Virginia Military Institute, served as a captain of the Richmond Grays. Manarin and Wallace, *Richmond Volunteers*, 248.

13. Charles A. McEvoy, an ordnance expert. He designed a cartridge for use in rifles that, despite these promising early assessments, could not endure the rigors of field service. One member of Company F wrote that "the solder on his cartridge needs strengthening and the copper foil which interlaces at the bottom should…also hold stronger; they are not quite strong enough to stand the jar of marching especially at the double quick." After these early efforts at small arms, McEvoy received appointment to the Confederate States Navy and worked in the Bureau of Ordnance and Hydrography on a number of fuses, sabots, percussion caps, and igniters. C. G. Chamberlayne, *Ham Chamberlayne-Virginian: Letters and Papers of an Artillery Officer in the War for Southern Independence 1861-1865* (Richmond, VA: Press of the Dietz Printing Co., 1932), 32; *Register of Officers of the Confederate States Navy 1861-1865*, rev. ed. (Washington, D.C.: Government Printing Office, 1931), 123; and, George M. Brooke, Jr., *Ironclads and Big Guns of the Confederacy: The Journal and Letters of John M. Brooke* (Columbia: University of South Carolina Press, 2002), 117, 119, 120, 121-122, 148, 152-153, 187.

14. President Lincoln had called for 75,000 troops to put down secession, with around 3,000 of them to come from Virginia.

15. Alexander Hugh Holmes Stuart and John Brown Baldwin who had been leading Unionists, like many other Upper South Unionists, shifted to support secession after Lincoln's call for troops. For more on the position of Upper South Unionists, see: Crofts, *Reluctant Confederates*, 308-352.

16. Charlie Crane and Mr. Royster were fellow boarders at the Johnson household.

17. John Minor Botts, the Virginia politician, despite Tucker's thoughts here, remained a staunch Unionist.

18. A rumor; Winfield Scott and Robert E. Lee were the two most famous Virginians in the United States Army. Winfield Scott would remain loyal to the Union, while Lee would resign.

19. The Virginia Convention went into a secret session to consider secession in the wake of Fort Sumter and Lincoln's call for troops.

20. From Matthew 24:6, King James Bible: "And ye shall hear of wars and rumours of wars: see that ye be not troubled: for all these things must come to pass, but the end is not yet."

21. Rocketts Landing was the docks just south of Richmond on the James River.

22. Steamships for the New York and Old Dominion line. *Jamestown* would be converted into a Confederate gunboat, while *Yorktown* would be renamed *Patrick Henry*. *Patrick Henry* would become the receiving ship for the Confederate Naval Academy in Richmond. Tucker's uncle, John R. Tucker, would create a James River Squadron for Virginia with *Patrick Henry* as the nucleus. After a little more than a month in existence, the Virginia State Navy became part of the Confederate States Navy. Ed Bearss, *River of Lost Opportunities: The Civil War on the James River 1861-1862* (Lynchburg, VA: H. E. Howard, 1995), 1-2.

23. A revolver manufactured by Remington based on a patent held by Fodyce Beals. William B. Edwards, *Civil War Guns* (Harrisburg, PA: The Stackpole Company, 1962), 192-193.

24. A large hotel at 8th and Main Streets in Richmond.

25. Erroneously reported; Scott remained loyal.

26. John S. Carlile, a prominent Unionist. Expelled from the Virginia Convention because of his strong Unionist bent, he attempted to send a telegram to Lincoln warning about the impending passage of Virginia's Ordinance of Secession. Carlile fled, but was captured near Fredericksburg. William H. Gaines, Jr., *Biographical Register of Members: Virginia State Convention of 1861 First Session* (Richmond: Library of Virginia, 1969), 25.

27. John Randolph Tucker, a United States Navy commander in Norfolk, tendered his resignation on April 18. The United States Navy dismissed him from service, to date from his resignation. Several days later, Governor Letcher gave Tucker command of the James River defenses. A commission as commander in the Virginia Navy, then in the Confederate Navy, followed. David P. Werlich, *Admiral of the Amazon: John Randolph Tucker, His Confederate Colleagues, and Peru* (Charlottesville: University Press of Virginia, 1990), 19-24.

28. When the 6th Massachusetts Infantry Regiment passed through Baltimore on its way to Washington, an angry mob assembled. Cheering for South Carolina and Jefferson Davis, the mob pelted the soldiers with paving stones and bricks. Soldiers also reported pistol and rifle fire. The Massachusetts troops opened fire to protect themselves. Four soldiers died and several dozen others were wounded. More than a dozen citizens of Baltimore were killed. George W. Nason, *Minute Men of '61 who Responded to the First Call of President Abraham Lincoln…: History and Complete Roster of the Massachusetts Regiments* (Boston: Smith & McCance, 1910), 196-199.

29. Robert A. Grannis, a clerk who boarded at the Johnson household along with Tucker.

30. Captain Charles McCauley ordered all ships at Norfolk scuttled on the night of April 20; Virginia troops entered the Navy yard and took possession the following morning. Werlich, *Admiral of the Amazon*, 21.

31. Steam-sloop USS *Pawnee*, rumored to be on its way to shell Richmond. Emory M. Thomas, *The Confederate State of Richmond: A Biography of the Capital* (Austin: University of Texas Press, 1971), 34-35.

32. Colonel Lewis Tilghman Moore commanded a regiment of Virginia Troops from Winchester. Robert K. Krick, *Lee's Colonels: A Biographical Register of the Field Officers of the Army of Northern Virginia*, 5ᵗʰ Ed., Rev. (Wilmington, NC: Broadfoot Publishing Company, 2009), 280.

33. Wilton, the historic Randolph family plantation on the James River

34. The Richmond Howitzers Artillery had been raised in the wake of John Brown's raid on Harper's Ferry in November 1859 and were Company H in the 1st Regiment Virginia Volunteers, along with Company F. The Howitzers first commander was Captain George Wythe Randolph, later to serve briefly as the Confederate Secretary of War. Lee A. Wallace, Jr., *A Guide to Virginia Military Organizations 1861-1865*, Rev. 2nd Ed. (Lynchburg, VA: H. E. Howard, 1986), 10.

35. The Richmond Fayette Artillery, another Richmond artillery unit, had been attached to the 1st Virginia Volunteers. Wallace, *A Guide to Virginia Military Organizations*, 3.

36. The Randolph family sold Wilton in 1859 to Colonel William C. Knight.

37. The Watkins family owned Ampthill Estate, across the river from Wilton. [Fairfax Harrison,] *The Virginia Carys: An Essay in Genealogy* (New York: De Vinne Press, 1919), 85n2.

38. Richard Milton Cary, a lawyer in civilian life. He would soon be promoted to colonel of the 30th Virginia Infantry Regiment in June. Krick, *Lee's Colonels*, 84.

39. Charley Crane, another boarder at the Johnston house.

40. The Richmond Light Infantry Blues. Organized in 1793, the Blues wore distinctive blue uniforms and fancy shakos. At this time, they were Company E of the 1st Virginia Regiment. At Fredericksburg, Captain R. Milton Cary, as senior captain of the two of the companies, led them both in drill. John A. Cutchins, *A Famous Command: The Richmond Light Infantry Blues* (Richmond, VA: Garrett & Massie, 1934), 73.

41. That is, the Richmond Light Infantry Blues. Tucker habitually abbreviates them to the "Bs" or "Blues."

42. Privates Robert C. White and John L. Cowardin. Worsham, *One of Jackson's Foot Cavalry*, 197, 206.

43. West Pointer Daniel Ruggles, originally from Massachusetts, had married a Virginian. During the early days of the Civil War, he held responsibility for Virginia defenses along the Potomac River. Ezra Warner, *Generals in Gray: Lives of Confederate Commanders* (Baton Rouge: Louisiana State University Press, 1959), 265-66.

44. Captain Reuben Lindsay Walker commanded the Purcell Artillery, which was stationed at Pratt's Point so that it could fend off Union gunboats. No man named Crump appears to have been formally mustered into the battery. Peter S. Carmichael, *The Purcell, Crenshaw and Letcher Artillery* (Lynchburg, VA: H. E. Howard, 1990), 3-5.

Chapter 2

1. On 22 April, Gov. John Letcher sent Capt. Walker of the Purcell Artillery along with four rifled 6-pounders to for duty at Aquia. Then-Virginia Major General Robert E. Lee dispatched two 8-inch columbiad artillery pieces, along with "implements and one hundred rounds of ammunition," on 24 April, which arrived at Aquia two days later on 26 April. R. E. Lee to Philip St. George Cocke, April 24,

1861, *The War of the Rebellion: A Compilation of the Official Records of the Union and Confederate Armies*, 128 vols. (Washington, DC: Government Printing Office, 1880-1901), Series, 1, Vol. 2, 777; and, Philip St. George Cocke to R. E. Lee, April, 26 1861, *OR* 2:780. Hereafter, citations will all begin with *OR*, with the volume given, part given in parentheses if applicable, followed by colon and the page number.

2. A reference to the fact that this battery had been laid out by naval personnel on shore; the battery at Aquia Creek Railroad Landing had been laid out by Virginia Maj. Thomas H. Williamson working alongside Virginia State Navy Captain William F. Lynch. Thomas H. Williamson to Daniel Ruggles, May 4, 1861, *OR* 2:811-812; Thomas H. Williamson to Brigadier General Daniel Ruggles, May 6, 1861, *OR* 2:812; and Daniel Ruggles to R. S. Garnett, May 8, 1861, *OR* 2:820.

3. Captain William F. Lynch and Lieutenant Charles C. Simms, both of the Virginia State Navy and later the Confederate States Navy. Both had resigned from the US Navy in April. William S. Dudley, *Going South: U.S. Navy Officer Resignations and Dismissals on the Eve of the Civil War* (Washington, DC: Naval Historical Foundation, 1981), 33, 38.

4. Private Mann Page.

5. The small Virginia State Naval forces steamer *George Page*.

6. Lieutenant John F. Alexander, of the Fredericksburg Artillery, had been detailed for special duties with the naval batteries on Aquia Creek. Robert K. Krick, *The Fredericksburg Artillery* (Lynchburg, VA: H. E. Howard, 1986), 97.

7. The official Confederate report noted that the Union steamers fired around fourteen shot and shell, while the Confederate artillery replied

with a dozen rounds. Daniel Ruggles to R. S. Garnett, May 30, 1861, *OR* 2:55.

8. While F Company had been sent to the Potomac River batteries, the bulk of the 1st Virginia Regiment had departed on May 24 for the vicinity of Manassas. Charles T. Loehr, *History of the Old First Virginia Infantry Regiment, Army of Northern Virginia* (Richmond: Wm. Ellis Jones, 1884), 7-8.

9. Tucker sought to serve as a commissioned officer, and had asked his father to help him seek a commission.

10. Commander James H. Ward led the steamers *Thomas Freeborn, Anacostia,* and *Resolute* against the Virginia forces at Aquia Creek. Though part of the same Potomac Flotilla, *Pawnee* was not involved in this engagement. Ward was unhurt in this fight, though he would be mortally wounded in action against the batteries at Mathias Point on June 27. Mary Alice Wills, *The Confederate Blockade of Washington, D.C. 1861-1862* (Parsons, WVA: McClain Printing Company, 1975), 25-26, 36-39.

11. Lieutenant Philip A. Wellford. Worhsam, *One of Jackson's Foot Cavalry*, 206.

12. In Greek mythology, the personification of darkness.

13. Richard H. Cunningham, Jr.

14. Richard F. Robinson. Worsham, *One of Jackson's Foot Cavalry*, 204.

15. According to John Worsham, both the 1st Arkansas Infantry Regiment and Walker's Tennessee Legion camped near Company F in Fredericksburg. Worsham, *One of Jackson's Foot Cavalry*, 7.

16. Former Virginia Governor Henry A. Wise raised a legion for service in Western Virginia. Manarin and Wallace, *Richmond Volunteers*, 264.

17. Because Tucker was under 18, he required his father's permission to enlist. On 26 June, Governor John Letcher directed Inspector General J. B. Baldwin to muster Tucker into service. Douglas Southall Freeman, *A Calendar of Confederate Papers with a Bibliography of Some Confederate Publications* (Richmond, VA: The Confederate Museum, 1908), 329.

18. The Madison Infantry mustered into service on May 23, 1861 and served in that capacity until converting into the Madison Light Artillery in August 1861. Arthur W. Bergeron, Jr., *Guide to Louisiana Confederate Military Units 1861–1865* (Baton Rouge: Louisiana State University Press, 1989), 34.

19. The weaving department of the State Penitentiary in Richmond caught fire, and F Company rushed to the scene through heavy rain and the resulting mud. Worsham, *One of Jackson's Foot Cavalry*, 10.

20. Up until this point in the war, F Company had retained its identity as part of the 1st Virginia Militia Regiment. With the organization and formalization of the Confederate Army, F Company mustered into Confederate service, rather than Virginia state service, on July 1, 1861. After its muster into Confederate service, F Company became company F in the 21st Virginia Infantry Regiment, with Colonel William Gilham in command. The Baltimore or Maryland Guard, which had also drilled alongside F Company at Camp Lee, became Company B of the 21st Virginia Infantry Regiment. Wallace, *A Guide to Virginia Military Organizations*, 103.

21. On July 11, Brigadier General William Starke Rosecrans attacked Lieutenant Colonel John Pegram's forces at Rich Mountain, near Beverly, Virginia. Using a local trail, Rosecrans flanked Pegram and broke the Confederate position. Some of Pegram's men managed to escape, but Pegram himself and more than five hundred Confederate remained trapped. They surrendered to Rosecran's commander, Major General George B. McClellan, on July 13. Brigadier General Robert S. Garnett, in overall command of the Confederate forces, fell back

due to the collapse of Pegram's position. During the retreat, Garnett became the first general officer to die during the Civil War when he was mortally wounded near Corrick's Ford on July 13. Walter S. Griggs, Jr., *General John Pegram C. S. A.* (Lynchburg, VA: H. E. Howard, 1993), 28-38; William M. Lamers, *The Edge of Glory: A Biography of General William S. Rosecrans, U.S.A.* (New York: Harcourt, Brace & World, 1961), 27-35; and, Warner, *Generals in Gray*, 100.

Chapter 3

1. Confederate forces led by P. G. T. Beauregard and Joseph E. Johnston defeated Union forces at the Battle of Manassas, or Bull Run on July 21.

2. John Worsham, another soldier in F Company, remarked on hearing the artillery fire at Manassas, recalling "the firing was as distinct that day as any I heard afterwards that was five to six miles off." Government authorities reassigned one of the wagons assigned to F Company and the driver of another refused to go further, necessitating the abandonment of some of the mess chests. Worsham, *One of Jackson's Foot Cavalry*, 14.

3. William Campbell Scott had been a colonel in the Virginia militia before becoming colonel of the 44th Virginia Infantry Regiment in June 1861. He had been present at the Confederate defeat at Rich Mountain and the locals likely blamed him for his part in the Confederate failure. Krick, *Lee's Colonels*, 338.

4. McClellan had departed for Washington, D.C., after the Union defeat at Bull Run, leaving Rosecrans in command of the Department of the Ohio. Lamers, *Edge of Glory*, 39.

5. Jesse Spinner Burks received colonecy of the 42nd Virginia Infantry Regiment in July 1861. Krick, *Lee's Colonels*, 72.

6. Colonel Gilham commanded a brigade composed of the 21st Virginia Infantry, the 42nd Virginia Infantry, the 48th Virginia Infantry, and the Irish Battalion. The Irish Battalion was also known as the 1st Battalion, Virginia Regulars. Susan A. Riggs, *21st Virginia Infantry* (Lynchburg, VA: H. E. Howard, 1991), 5.

7. John Mercer Patton, Jr., had been promoted to Lieutenant Colonel of the 21st Virginia Infantry in June 1861. Krick, *Lee's Colonels*, 300-301.

8. Brigadier General William W. Loring, a veteran of war against the Seminoles and the Mexican-American War, received command of the Army of Northwestern Virginia on July 20. R. E. Lee to W. W. Loring, July 20, 1861, in *OR* 2:986; and, Warner, *Generals in Gray*, 193-194.

9. Picket duty entailed standing guard in an advanced position, watching for the enemy. Soldiers on picket duty would also challenge those passing to ensure that they were friendly and would raise an alarm if the enemy was sighted.

10. David B. Jones. Worsham *One of Jackson's Foot Cavalry*, 200.

11. Loring had lost his arm at the battle of Chapultepec during the Mexican-American War. Warner, *Generals in Gray*, 193. General Robert E. Lee took command of all the Confederate forces in Western Virginia, those of Loring along with others under John B. Floyd and Henry A. Wise. William Allan, *History of the Campaign of Gen. T. J. (Stonewall) Jackson in the Shenandoah Valley of Virginia* (Philadelphia: J.B. Lippincott, 1880), 13n1.

12. Virginia Military Institute graduate Scott Shipp served as the major of the 21st Virginia infantry Regiment. Later in the war, he commanded the VMI cadets during the battle of New Market. Krick, *Lee's Colonels*, 344.

13. Lieutenant Colonel Daniel Allen Langhorne, an 1845 graduate of the Virginia Military Institute. Krick, *Lee's Colonels*, 231.

14. Ham Chamberlayne, a member of F Company also on this expedition, noted as well that the F Company had pursued Yankee scouts, but "found the birds had flown." He also remarked on the "great breakfast" the men enjoyed. Chamberlayne, *Ham Chamberlayne--Virginian*, 30.

15. Ham Chamberlayne also wrote that the march back had been so exhausting, "we were almost too tired to eat." Chamberlayne, *Ham Chamberlayne--Virginian*, 30.

16. Captain Sherwood Mustain commanded Company H of the 21st Virginia Infantry. Riggs, *21st Virginia Infantry*, 83.

17. Sergeant George William Peterkin, later to become the first Episcopal bishop of West Virginia, recalled: "as long as I was up and about, and not out on picket duty, I attended the funerals of the men of our Brigade, and gave them the last rites of the Church." Robert Edward Lee Strider, *The Life and Work of George William Peterkin* (Philadelphia: George W. Jacobs & Company, 1929), 48.

18. John Worsham remembered of this period that "in all my experience of the war I never saw as much mud." Worsham, *One of Jackson's Foot Cavalry*, 17.

19. The 1st Tennessee Infantry Regiment. A member of the regiment wrote in his memoirs about how "a sudden volley of small arms resounded through the mountain, and some one, thinking the Federal forces had attacked General Lee's position, ordered the long roll beaten…every man seized his gun and cartridge box." Rushing off without much other equipment, "they reported for duty" and found "it was altogether a false alarm. A regiment had been on picket duty and was firing off guns in order to clean them." *Doctor Quintard: Chaplain C.S.A. and Second Bishop of Tennessee: The Memoir and Civil War Diary of Charles Todd Quintard*, ed. Sam Davis Elliott (Baton Rouge: Louisiana State University Press, 2003), 21-22.

20. Richard Morris Fontaine, who would be discharged in November 1861 due to the effects of typhoid fever. Worsham, *One of Jackson's Foot Cavalry*, 198.

21. Lieutenant Jake Hubbard of Company H. Riggs, *21st Virginia Infantry*, 76.

22. Privates John Worsham, John Powell, Richard MacMurdo, and Corporal Jesse Child. Worsham did not mention this sickness in his account of the Civil War. Worsham, *One of Jackson's Foot Cavalry*, 196, 201, 203.

23. Captain Cunningham.

24. Lieutenant Edward Mayo of F Company. Worsham, *One of Jackson's Foot Cavalry*, 201.

25. John J. Reeve of F Company. When the war broke out, Reeve was a student at the University of Virginia in Charlottesville, but he soon joined F Company in Richmond. He served with F Company until April 1862, when he received promotion and began service as a staff officer. Worsham, *One of Jackson's Foot Cavalry*, 203; *Confederate Military History: Volume XI: Kentucky*, extended ed. (1899; repr., Wilmington, NC: Broadfoot Publishing Company, 1988), 509.

26. John Worsham recalled that the skirmishing at Conrad's mill marked the time the men saw their "first dead Yankee. He made a lasting impression, his face upturned and a fresh pool of blood at his side, showing that his life had just passed away." Worsham, *One of Jackson's Foot Cavalry*, 17.

27. The Georgia Troop Artillery Battalion began the war as part of Cobb's Legion, but it served on detached duty with Gilham's brigade from September to November 1861. Stewart Sifakis, *Compendium of the Confederate Armies: South Carolina and Georgia* (New York: Facts on File, 1995), 144-45.

28. Colonel John Augustine Washington, a great nephew of George Washington and aide-de-camp to General Lee, received a mortal wound from 10-pounder Parrott shell from Loomis' Battery. Robert E. L. Krick, *Staff Officers in Gray: A Biographical Register of the Staff Officers in the Army of Northern Virginia* (Chapel Hill: University of North Carolina Press, 2003), 297; and, *OR* 5:185-186.

29. Lieutenant Henry T. Miller of F Company. Worsham, *One of Jackson's Foot Cavalry*, 201.

30. Captain Thomas B. Robinson's Company G. Wallace, *A Guide to Virginia Military Organizations*, 103.

31. US President Abraham Lincoln's initial call for troops had specified a period of enlistment not to exceed three months, in order to comply with the 1795 Militia Act. Troops who mustered in as 3-months volunteers could reenlist after the initial term of service for a longer duration.

32. Sergeant Thomas Ellet. Worsham. *One of Jackson's Foot Cavalry*, 198.

33. Private Daniel D. Talley of F Company. Worsham, *One of Jackson's Foot Cavalry*, 205.

34. Captain Francis Deane Irving, of Company D. Riggs, *21st Virginia Infantry*, 77.

35. Col. Gilham, after falling back from Valley Mountain to Middle Mountain, decided to relocate from Middle Mountain to Elk Mountain. The events Tucker describes here took place on September 28. Worsham, *One of Jackon's Foot Cavalry*, 18.

36. At this time, several different privates named Moore served in the 21st Virginia Infantry, so this stuck individual must have been either Elijah Moore, John Moore, Samuel Moore, or William J. Moore. Riggs, *21st Virginia Infantry*, 82.

37. Robert T. Coleman, the surgeon of the 21st Virginia Infantry.

38. F Company private Christopher A. Robinson. Worsham, *One of Jackson's Foot Cavalry*, 204.

39. On October 3, Union forces made an armed reconnaissance on Confederate positions on the Greenbrier River. Confederate Brigadier General Henry R. Jackson wrote of the engagement that "after a hot fire of four and half hours, and heavy attempts to charge our lines, [the enemy] was repulsed, evidently with considerable loss." The Federal commander, Brigadier General Joseph J. Reynolds, for his part, stated that "we...made a thorough reconnaissance, and after having fully and successfully accomplished the object of the expedition retired leisurely and in good order." Reynolds, like Jackson, thought that he had inflicted heavy casualties on the other side. In reality, the Union suffered 43 casualties while Confederate losses numbered 52. See *OR* 5:220-236.

40. Members of Tucker's mess, who had formed the "*Pawnee* mess;" see diary entry for April 26, 1861.

41. Private William Exall of F Company. Worsham, *One of Jackson's Foot Cavalry*, 198.

42. Unknown what this message references. Rosecrans had withdrawn from his positions on Big Sewell Mountain on October 5, preventing Confederate forces from attacking on October 6. Otherwise, no major events took place in the theater in mid-October. Lamers, *Edge of Glory*, 53-57.

43. Brigadier General Samuel Read Anderson, a veteran of the Mexican American War, commanded a brigade composed of the 1st, 7th, and 14th Tennessee Infantry Regiments. *OR* 5:770; and Warner, *Generals in Gray*, 10.

44. Lieutenant Colonel John Mercer Patton of the 21st Virginia Infantry Regiment. Krick, *Lee's Colonels*, 300-301.

45. Captain James Gardiner Paxton was appointed assistant quartermaster at Jackson's River on September 17, 1862. Krick, *Staff Officers in Gray*, 238.

46. See Tucker's diary entry of September 15, where it seems that Loring had attempted to motivate the men by saying they would either take Baltimore or die. In this passage, Tucker suggests that due to the weather, many in the army would die and that no one would make it to Baltimore, unless they were captured by the Federals and sent there as a prisoner of war.

47. Lt. Col. Carter Littlepage Stevenson of Fredericksburg, Virginia, served as Loring's assistant adjutant general from July 21, 1861. [Marcus J. Wright,] *List of Staff Officers of the Confederate States Army*, with a new introduction by John M. Carroll (reprint; Mattituck, NY: J.M. Carroll, [1891] 1983), 156; Warner, *Generals in Gray*, 292-93.

48. From Shakespeare's *Hamlet*, Act 1, Scene IV. In the scene, two guards and Hamlet discuss corruption in the kingdom before the appearance of the ghost of Hamlet's father.

49. Lieutenant Thomas A. Hancock. John Worsham related this event in his memoir. After chasing the deer, he found himself under arrest, as "an order had been issues to the guard to arrest every man found with a gun in his hand." Worsham claimed that "I was the only man arrested." Worsham, *One of Jackson's Foot Cavalry*, 21.

50. Private Robert M. Tabb. Worsham, *One of Jackson's Foot Cavalry*, 205.

51. Sergeant Edward J. Rawlings, Jr. Worsham, *One of Jackson's Foot Cavalry*, 203.

52. Tucker imputes that African-American vernacular used the word "big" in a sarcastic way, to apply to someone with an overly-inflated ego or sense of themselves.

53. Flatbed railroad cars.

54. Private John Edward Wambersie of Company B, 21st Virginia Infantry, the "Maryland Guard." Fellow Confederate Marylander McHenry Howard later claimed that: "Jack Wamberzie was said, while on picket, to have challenged and then fired the first Maryland shot of the war–at a lightning bug." McHenry Howard, *Recollections of a Maryland Confederate Soldier and Staff Officer Under Johnston, Jackson and Lee* (Baltimore: Williams & Wilkins, 1914), 22.

55. Virginians held general elections for Confederate officials on November 6. Troops in the field could vote, too, with a tent serving as the "voting precinct," and "all enlisted soldiers of good standing, regardless of age, could vote," which they did "with much enthusiasm." The candidates Tucker refers to stood for a seat as a Virginia representative in the Confederate House of Representatives. The voting totals here mirror that of the election overall, where former U.S. president John Tyler defeated James Lyons and W. H. MacFarland. When Tyler died in 1862, Lyons successfully stood to replace him. Worsham, *One of Jackson's Foot Cavalry*, 20-21; Ezra J. Warner and W. Buck Yearns, *Biographical Register of the Confederate Congress* (Baton Rouge: Louisiana State University Press, 1975), 155.

56. First Lieutenant Edward Mayo resigned, with William P. Wellford elected to the first lieutenancy. This opened the second lieutenancy. William Granville Gray, Jr., James B. Payne, Jr., and Charles Robert Skinker stood for the position. Worsham, *One of Jackson's Foot Cavalry*, 22.

57. Reverend William Sparrow removed to Staunton Virginia after the Federal occupation of Alexandria, Virginia. He had been teaching at the Virginia Theological Seminary and attempted to reestablish it in

Confederate Virginia. Cornelius Walker, *The Life and Correspondence of Rev. William Sparrow, D.D.* (Philadelphia: James Hammond, 1876), 248-50.

58. The Western State Lunatic Asylum, established in 1828.

59. Colonel Thomas Pearson August, former colonel of the 1st Virginia Volunteers (militia), commanded the 15th Virginia Infantry Regiment. Krick, *Lee's Colonels*, 37.

60. Lieutenant Henry Miller resigned to become assistant adjutant general of the 26th Virginia Infantry. Prviate William Granville Gray Jr. and Sergeant John Pizzini stood to take his place. Riggs, *21st Virginia Infantry*, 82.

61. Captain J. Lyle Clarke of Company B. Riggs, *21st Virginia Infantry*, 64.

62. Rev. George Boardman Taylor, a Baptist preacher from Staunton. His brother served in Company F. He had preached a sermon to F Company in September, Chamberlayne, *Ham Chamberlayne-Virginian*, 34, 37.

63. Private T. Ritchie Green. Worsham, *One of Jackson's Foot Cavalry*, 199.

64. In November 1861, a US Navy vessel stopped and boarded a British mail steamer and took off of it James Mason and John Sliddell, two Confederate diplomats. The action provoked a diplomatic incident because the two were taken from a neutral vessel, contrary to international law. Eventually the US released Mason and Slidell in order to mollify the British. See *Autobiography of Charles Wilkes, U.S. Navy 1798-1877*, ed. William James Morgan, et al. (Washington, DC: Naval History Division, 1978), 767-781.

65. Lieutenant Colonel George Woodson Hansborough had been wounded at Alleghany Mountain. He wrote that "whilst descending from a log on which I had been standing for a moment urging the men forward to the charge, I was prostrated by a pistol ball, which entered my right thigh." Krick, *Lee's Colonels*, 176; and "Report of Lieut. Col. G. W. Hansbrough, C.S. Army," *OR* 5:466.

66. A Sibley Tent; then the main field shelter issued to Confederate troops.

67. An election for officers of the regiment. Elected 1st and 2nd lieutenant, respectively, were Philip Alexander Wellford and James B. Payne, Jr.

68. Colonel John Arthur Campbell commanded the 48th Virginia Infantry Regiment. Krick, *Lee's Colonels*, 78.

69. Captain Lawrence S. Marye's Hampden Artillery, organized in Richmond and named after the English statesman John Hampden (1594-1643), a leader of Parliament who opposed Charles I. Wallace, *A Guide to Virginia Military Organizations*, 9.

70. The mince pie went unremarked upon by John Worsham, who recalled catching sight of Stonewall Jackson for the first time on Christmas day–"His head was covered by a faded gray cap, pulled down so far over his face that between cap and whiskers was very little to see. Yet as we passed we caught a glimpse of pair of dark flashing eyes from underneath the brim of his cap"–and the general bounty of the Shenandoah Valley–"every house had sausage, spare ribs, chine, liver, etc. to give us." Worsham, *One of Jackson's Foot Cavalry*, 23, 24.

71. Private John H. Ellerson. Worsham, *One of Jackson's Foot Cavalry*, 197.

72. Brigadier General Benjamin Franklin Kelley commanded a Union division tasked with protecting the Baltimore and Ohio Railroad. He

occupied Romney, Virginia in October 1861. Tucker's statement that Kelley was on the march with 15,000 troops was just a rumor. Kelley, however, advocated aggressive action, as did his subordinate, Brigadier General Frederick Lander. Theodore F. Lang, *Loyal West Virginia from 1861 to 1865* (Baltimore: The Deutsch Publishing Company, 1895), 320-322; Richard A. Sauers, *The Devastating Hand of War: Romney, West Virginia, During the Civil War* (Shepherd College: The George Tyler Moore Center for the Study of the Civil War, 2000), 15-16; and, Gary L. Ecelbarger, *Frederick W. Lander: The Great Natural American Soldier* (Baton Rouge: Louisiana State University Press, 2000), 197.

73. John Worsham, long after the war, claimed that the 21st Virginia Infantry Regiment actually possessed a mixture of weapons, from Springfields, Enfields, and Mississippi rifles, among other arms. Worsham, *One of Jackson's Foot Cavalry*, 60.

74. Captain William Nelson Pendleton had organized the Rockbridge Artillery in May 1861; Captain Lindsay V. Shumaker's Danville (Virginia) Artillery, Wallace, *Guide to Virginia Military Organizations*, 21, 30.

Chapter 4

1. Thomas M. Rankin, *Stonewall Jackson's Romney Campaign January 1-February 20, 1862* (Lynchburg, VA: H.E. Howard, 1994), 61-62, 81-98;. Sauers, *The Devastating Hand of War*, 23-40.

2. Lt. Colonel Seth M. Barton of the 3rd Arkansas Infantry Regiment. Warner, *Generals in Gray*, 18.

3. At this skirmish near Bath, the Federals reported losses of 3 wounded and 8 captured. Payne, promoted to lieutenant only on December 28, 1861, would leave the service due to his injuries. Worsham, *One of Jackson's Foot Cavalry*, 25, 25n, 202.

4. Tucker means the tangle with the scouting party mentioned in the previous paragraph.

5. The "General" must have been Loring. Stonewall Jackson had been more nonplussed about the skirmish, In his report of the affair, he complained that "Colonel Gilham, while moving with his brigade in the direction of Sir John's Run Depot, came up with the enemy, but as he neither attacked them nor notified me of the cause of not doing so, nor even of his overtaken the Federal forces, their artillery and infantry were permitted to escape." "Report of Maj. Gen. Thomas J. Jackson, C.S. Army, of operations from November 4, 1861, to February 21, 1862," in *OR* 5:391.

6. On January 4, Colonel Albert Rust led his regiment (3rd Arkansas Infantry) and the 37th Virginia Infantry Regiment, along with two guns of the Shumaker (Danville) Battery to destroy the railway bridge over the Great Cacapon (or Big Cacapon) River. There, "the guard made stout resistance." Allan, *History of the Campaign of Gen. T. J. (Stonewall) Jackson in the Shenandoah Valley of Virginia*, 22; and "Reports of Maj. Gen. Thomas J. Jackson, C.S. Army, of operations from November 4, 1861, to February 21, 1862," in *OR* 5:390.

7. Carter L. Stevenson, a staff officer, would be promoted to colonel of the 53rd Virginia Infantry Regiment, a position he held only briefly until his promotion to brigadier general in February 1862. Warner, *Generals in Gray*, 293.

8. That is, disabled the artillery pieces by breaking a piece of metal off in the vent hole. With the metal filling the vent hole, the piece could not be fired until the vent hole had been drilled out.

9. Gilham, a former instructor at the Virginia Military Institute, and Ship had been ordered to serve on the faculty at VMI. Krick, *Lee's Colonels*, 154, 344.

10. The phrase "Here's your mule" was a comic call "none more widespread and generally used among the Confederates." Some claimed it originated in a camp of instruction in Tennessee, where soldiers hid a sutler's mule. Soldiers then yelled "Here's your mule" at various points, while others watched and laughed as the sutler frantically ran back and forth trying to find his animal. After that supposed initial usage, the cry "spread rapidly through the army, until it was in general use by soldiers who had no idea of how it originated, but understood that there was a joke behind it or connected with it in some way." Here the joke seems to be that Tucker and his compatriots gave a fine horse to Col. Gilham but poked fun at its expense by shouting "Here's your mule." W. W. Carnes, "'Here's Your Mule'," in Bromfield L. Ridley, *Battles and Sketches of the Army of Tennessee* (Mexico, MO: Missouri Printing & Publishing Co., 1906), 632-634.

11. Jackson was notorious for granting few leaves of absence for his troops. James I. Robertson, Jr., *Stonewall Jackson: The Man, the Soldier, the Legend* (New York: MacMillan Publishing, 1997), 300, 311.

12. Philip A. Wellford

13. Richard H. Cunningham, Jr.

14. The 1st Georgia Infantry Regiment (Ramsey's), the only Georgia unit with the 21st Virginia Infantry Regiment in Loring's army.

15. Tucker's statistics do not much exaggerate the extent of the misery and attrition. Colonel Samuel Fulkerson of the 37th Virginia Infantry Regiment, in Loring's army, wrote that the harsh campaign had "emaciated the force almost to a skeleton, compared to what it was on marching from" Winchester. A letter from Loring's commanding officers, including the commander of the 1st Georgia Infantry Regiment, noted "that some regiments which left Winchester with nearly 600 men should now, short as the time has been, report less than 200 men for duty." Samuel V. Fulkerson to Walter R. Staples,

January 23, 1862 in *OR* 5:1041; and William B. Taliaferro, et. al., to Brigadier-General Loring, January 25, 1862, in *OR* 5:1047.

16. Many early Confederate enlistments had enlisted for only twelve months. By December, the Confederate Congress realized that the war would continue longer than that. It passed an act on December 11, which offered soldiers a bounty of $50 and a two month's furlough if the soldiers would enlist for either two year, three years, or the duration of the war. Albert Burton Moore, *Conscription and Conflict in the Confederacy* (New York: Macmillan, 1924), 6-7.

17. April 21 was the end of the initial one year term of enlistment of F Company.

18. Private Edmond "Ned" Tompkins. Riggs, *21st Virginia Infantry*, 94.

19. The 21st Virginia Infantry billeted in the town of Romney. While most of the men lodged in deserted houses, F Company stayed in the bank. John Worhsam recollected that "we lived well there." His "mess employed an old darky, about two squares off, to cook our rations. She added to them any good thing she could get." Worsham also enjoyed the buckwheat cakes, butter, and syrup that a nearby hotel served for breakfast. Worsham, *One of Jackson's Foot Cavalry*, 28.

20. Kentucky whiskey. This mention, perhaps, constitutes an instance of the stereotype of the Irish being inordinately fond of liquor, as the Regulars were also known as the "Irish Battalion."

21. Union troops under Col. S. H. Dunning routed a Confederate outpost at Hanging Rock Gap (also Blue's Gap) on January 7, 1862. Due to the fact that buildings in the area had been used to house Confederate troops, Dunning ordered them put to the torch. Rankin, *Stonewall Jackson's Romney Campaign*, 108-109, 113, 135.

22. Sergeant Aaron W. Ernull and Prviate E. Peyton Hodson, both of Company B. According to Tucker's letter of February 9, 1862, they died of pneumonia. Riggs, *21st Virginia*, 70, 76.

23. Reverend Charles T. Quintard, chaplain of the 1st Tennessee Infantry Regiment. Like many others, Quintard noted the hardships of the Romney Campaign. Perhaps a number of funerals such as this one led him to remember "that we were subject to the severest trials that human nature could endure." Elliott, *Doctor Quintard*, 37.

24. Likely fellow F Company member Richard F. Robinson. Worsham, *One of Jackson's Foot Cavalry*, 204.

25. The aforementioned Aaron W. Ernull and E. Peyton Hodson.

26. Private Joseph N. Willis of F Company. Worsham, *One of Jackson's Foot Cavalry*, 206.

27. Robert T. Coleman, the regimental surgeon.

28. Others thought that Jackson had much to answer for, too. Complaints had reached a crescendo and made their way to Richmond. There, on January 31, Confederate Secretary of War Judah P. Benjamin ordered Jackson to pull Loring's troops back to Winchester. Jackson, incensed that his command had been interfered with, resigned. Governor Letcher and his aide Alexander Boteler managed to smooth matters over, and Jackson withdrew his resignation letter. One of Jackson's staff officers noted after the war that: "Indeed, it is difficult to realize the feeling of distrust then manifested, when we consider the unbounded enthusiasm and devotion with which many of these same men afterwards followed Jackson to victory and death." Allan, *History of the Campaign of T.J. (Stonewall) Jackson*, 29.

29. After Jackson withdrew his resignation letter, he went on the offensive. He pushed for a court-martial of Loring on seven different specifications. The Confederate government, tired of the entire affair,

promoted Loring and moved him away from Jackson. Loring was likely not actually put under arrest. Robertson, *Stonewall Jackson*, 320-321.

30. While Tucker could not purchase a commission outright, he could fund the outfitting of a company with the expectation that the men would elect him their officer after mustering in. In this letter, Tucker observes that it would be too expensive to take that course of action.

31. Ellet evidently put the information on reenlistment to good use. Shortly after this letter was written, he transferred to the artillery and was soon elected lieutenant. *Confederate Military History: Vol. 4: Virginia*, extended edition, (1899; reprint, Wilmington, NC: Broadfoot Publishing Company, 1987), 854.

32. Overall, disease accounted for two-thirds of soldier deaths during the Civil War. For more on how soldiers in this time period thought of disease and health, see Kathryn Shively Meier, *Nature's Civil War: Common Soldiers and the Environment in 1862 Virginia* (Chapel Hill: University of North Carolina Press, 2013).

33. Presumably one of the enslaved people who Tucker's family owned.

34. In February 1862, Richmond businessman William G. Crenshaw, and others, announced the recruitment of a new artillery battery. Carmichael, *The Purcell, Crenshaw and Letcher Artillery*, 58.

35. Beyond the acts passed by the Confederate Congress, Virginia legislators passed an act in early February 1862 to strengthen Confederate manpower. Under this act, all white males between the ages of 18 and 45 would be liable to conscription; however, if they voluntarily enlisted before then, they would be able to choose their branch of service and elect their officers. Stonewall Jackson took a dim view of the ongoing reorganization, viewing it as a fiasco that seriously undermined his strength. He also thought that permitting the election of officer would undermine efficiency, as the men would elect

popular men rather than those who preferred the necessary discipline. Robertson, *Stonewall Jackson: The Man, The Soldier, The Legend*, 327.

36. Sergeant George G. Gibson of Company B. Riggs, *21st Virginia*, 72.

37. Federal troops advanced from Berryville to just north of Winchester. Jackson had his men construct breastworks and block the advance along the Berryville Road. In the event, the Federals stopped short of the Confederate troops. Gary L. Ecelbarger, *"We are in for it!": The First Battle of Kernstown* (Shippensburg, PA: White Mane Publishing Company, 1997), 45-47.

38. As Stonewall Jackson moved south, Colonel Turner Ashby's 7th Virginia Cavalry patrolled closer to Winchester. During and after Banks's advance, "Ashby, with his cavalry, had kept up an incessant activity." Thomas M. Ashby, *Life of Turner Ashby* (New York: Neale Publishing, 1914), 130; and, Ecelbarger, *"We are in for it!,"* 55-58.

39. For the most part, Jackson fell back unmolested by Union forces, permitting him to collect and bring with him supplies useful for waging war. Lowell Reidenbaugh, *Jackson's Valley Campaign: The Battle of Kernstown* (Lynchburg, VA: H. E. Howard, 1996), 57.

40. Francis Marion, a famous partisan leader of the American Revolution. Marion combined "Revolutionary legacy with the romance so important to the knight ideal." Many viewed Ashby in such terms. Paul Christopher Anderson, *Blood Image: Turner Ashby in the Civil War and the Southern Mind* (Baton Rouge: Louisiana State University Press, 2002), 125.

41. Brigadier General Edward "Alleghany" Johnson had received both his sobriquet and general's star after his victory at the battle of Alleghany Mountain in December. His command amounted to a brigade-size formation. Although Jackson had pressed Richmond to release Johnson's brigade to operate under his command, Johnson would not join Jackson until after the Battle of Kernstown, which took

place two days after Tucker wrote this letter. Johnson and his men would play an important role in Jackson's May 8 victory at McDowell, which inaugurated the string of successes that would become known as Jackson's Valley Campaign. Gregg S. Clemmer, *Old Alleghany: The Life and Wars of General Ed Johnson* (Staunton, VA: Hearthside Publishing Company, 2004), 337-414.

42. Ashby's cavalry had advanced along the Valley Pike and pushed almost into Winchester. There, they heard that only four Union regiments remained in Winchester. Ashby, thinking he could easily take the town, sent a messenger to Jackson asking for support. Thus did Jackson assume he could easily outmatch the Union forces nearby. Tucker vastly overstates Union losses here, as was common with initial reports. The most notable Union casualty was Brigadier General James Shields, who suffered a broken arm and injured shoulder from a shell fragment. Lowell Reidenbaugh, *The Battle of Kernstown*, 70-73; Ecelbarger, *"We are in for It!,"* 68-75.

Chapter 5

1. For thorough accounts of Kernstown, see Ecelbarger, *"We are In For It*; and Lowell Reidenbaugh, *Jackson's Valley Campaign: The Battle of Kernstown.*

2. Henry V. Picot later died of these wounds. Worsham, *One of Jackson's Foot Cavalry*, 202.

3. Malcolm N. Fleming, the assistant surgeon of the 21st Virginia Infantry. Riggs, *21st Virginia Infantry*, 71.

4. John Worsham recalled, "arriving at Middletown, I learned that Tucker Randolph, one of my messmates, was in one of the houses. Wounded, he had been sent to the rear the evening before. I soon found him and,

seeing the condition of my dear old comrade, I made up my mind to stay and nurse him." Worsham, *One of Jackson's Foot Cavalry*, 33-34.

5. John T. Weaver had been hit in the thigh. Riggs, *21st Virginia Infantry*, 96.

6. Worsham said he "had long ago made up my mind never to be taken prisoner, but I could not leave me messmate…I finally became so uneasy that I went to all the town folks to see if I could get a vehicle of some kind to take him away; but I could get nothing." Eventually, Worsham "saw an ambulance coming on a run. We put Randolph into it in a hurry, pitched in his knapsack, etc., and off we went." Worsham, *One of Jackson's Foot Cavalry*, 34.

7. John Worsham recalled "we could hear firing in the rear all day, and during the march" but no general engagement took place. Worsham, *One of Jackson's Foot Cavalry*, 35.

8. Lieutenant Colonel Alexander Galt Taliaferro commanded the 23rd Virginia Infantry Regiment. Tucker has misstated the opening of the Battle of Kernstown. The 27th Virginia Infantry under Colonel John Echols was the first infantry unit engaged, with the 21st Virginia Infantry supporting. A modern estimate puts the casualties of the 21st Virginia Infantry at 14 killed or mortally wounded and 37 wounded. Reidenbaugh, *Jackson's Valley Campaign: The Battle of Kernstown*, 72, 76; and Ecclebarger, *"We are in for It!"*, 274.

9. The Battle of Shiloh, 6-7 April, 1862. A Confederate army under Gen. Albert Sidney Johnston attacked Union forces under the command of Ulysses S. Grant. Johnston suffered a mortal wound on the first day of the battle.

Chapter 6

1. Richmond Dispatch, May 31, 1862, page 4, col 2. Governor John Letcher referred to Tucker as holding the rank of captain around this time, but that may have been contingent upon Tucker raising the artillery battery. Telegrams and Letters Received by the Confederate States War Department, 273-L-1862, Microfilm, Swem Library and Archives, College of William and Mary, Williamsburg, Virginia.

2. Earl J. Hess, *The Civil War in the West: Victory and Defeat from the Appalachians to the Mississippi* (Chapel Hill: University of North Carolina Press, 2012), 92-96.

Chapter 7

1. Hess, *The Civil War in the West*, 96-97; Joseph H. Parks, *General E. Kirby Smith C.S.A.* (Baton Rouge: Louisiana State University Press, 1954), 200-216

2. Brig. Gen. Henry Heth guarded the wagon trains for the invasion force. A Virginia veteran of the antebellum army, Heth had served in Western Virginia where he compiled a mixed record of victories and losses. In July 1862, he took command of four brigades in Kirby Smith's forces. At this time, Tucker rode with Col. Henry M. Ashby's 1st Tennessee Cavalry Regiment, which composed part of one of Heth's brigades. James L. Morrison Jr., editor, *The Memoirs of Henry Heth* (Westport, Ct.: Greenwood Press, 1974), 165; *OR* 16:2, 719.

3. Major General Edmund Kirby Smith's army fought an intense battle on August 30th at Richmond, Kentucky. The Confederates inflicted 5,353 casualties on the Federal force (including more than 4,303 prisoners) while losing only 624. Union Brigadier General Mahlon Manson was captured and would be exchange in December 1862. His superior officer, Major General William Bull Nelson received a

slight wound and recovered, only to be shot dead after a confrontation with fellow Union brigadier-general Jefferson C. Davis. Kenneth A. Hafendorfer, *The Battle of Richmond, Kentucky August 30, 1862* (Lousiville, KY: KH Press, 2006), 391-392, 397, 401, and *passim*; and Nathaniel Cheairs Hughes, Jr., and Gordon D. Whitney, *Jefferson Davis in Blue: The Life of Sherman's Relentless Warrior* (Baton Rouge: Louisiana State University Press, 2002), 100-126.

4. Col. Thomas Hamilton McCray, of the 31st Arkansas Infantry Regiment, commanded the First Brigade at the Richmond. Despite being "under a galling fire of bombs, rifle-shot, and Minie balls" so intense he described "finding the air literally filled" with them, McCray apparently suffered no wounds battle. *OR* 16(1):942; Bruce S. Allardice, *More Generals in Gray* (Baton Rouge: Louisiana State University Press, 1995), 158-59.

5. A "rifle ball" hit Brig. Gen. Patrick R. Cleburne in the left cheek and "carried away his teeth on that side." After the "wound deprived him of the power of speech," he left the field. He recovered by October 1862 and returned to his brigade. Irving A. Buck, *Cleburne and His Command*, edited by Thomas Robson Hay (repr., Jackson, Tn.: McCowat-Mercer Press, 1959 [1908]), 107, 110.

6. Union Brigadier General George Morgan evacuated from his position at Cumberland Gap on September 17. While in place, he had impeded Confederate communications. Kenneth A. Hafendorfer, *Perryville: Battle for Kentucky*, 2nd Ed. (Louisville, KY: KH Press, 1991), 30, 62.

7. Major Randolph Harrison Finney. Krick, *Staff Officers in Gray*, 128.

8. Tucker's younger brother, Norman, was born in 1846. In April 1862, at age 16, he joined Scott's Partisan Rangers, a cavalry unit in Virginia and served with it until October 1863. During his service with Scott's Rangers, he suffered a wound in a skirmish near Upperville in 1863. Norman's next confirmed service came in November 1864, when he joined John S. Mosby's command. [Jedediah Hotchkiss,] *Confederate*

Military History, Extended Edition: Vol. IV: Virginia (1899; reprint, Wilmington, NC: Broadfoot Publishing Company, 1987), 1133.

9. The 21st Virginia Infantry had been heavily engaged at the Battle of Cedar Mountain on 9 August, suffering nearly forty killed and almost ninety wounded. Ned Tompkins had been wounded "in the body and through one arm." John H. Worsham, *One of Jackson's Foot Cavalry*, ed. James I. Robertson, Jr. (repr.; Jackson, TN: McCowat-Mercer Press, 1964 [1912]), 66

10. Bragg won a victory at the Perryville, Kentucky on October 8. Despite defeating a large portion of the Union Army commanded by Major General Don Carlos Buell, Bragg and Kirby Smith found themselves at a strategic disadvantage. When taking up a new position to protect themselves, they abandoned a large part of their supplies. This necessitated a retreat back to Cumberland Gap and out of Kentucky. Hess, *The Civil War in the West*, 101-102.

11. Brig. Gen. Thomas J. Wood commanded a Union division.

12. The 1st Ohio Cavalry Regiment reported constant skirmishing during this period. W. L. Curry, *Four Years in the Saddle: History of the First Regiment Ohio Volunteer Cavalry* (Columbus, OH: Champlin Printing Company, 1898), 75-80.

13. Colonel Benjamin Allston, commander of the cavalry brigade of the Department of East Tennessee, had been wounded during a skirmish on October 8. Colonel Henry Marshall Ashby of the 2nd Tennessee Cavalry Regiment assumed command of the brigade. A Virginia, Ashby had attended the College of William and Mary, but did not graduate. His Civil War career followed a similar trajectory; although Ashby commanded brigades at various points during the war, he never received promotion to general. As Tucker indicates in the postscript to this letter, Ashby was, indeed, a cousin of Turner Ashby. Kenneth A. Hafendorfer, *They Died by Twos and Tens: The Confederate Cavalry in the Kentucky Campaign of 1862* (Louisville, KY: KH Press, 1995), 742;

Bruce S. Allardice, *More General in Gray* (Baton Rouge: Louisiana State University Press, 1995), 22-23; and James L. Mohon, "Defending the Confederate Heartland: Company F of Henry Ashby's 2nd Tennessee Cavalry," *Civil War Regiments: A Journal of the American Civil War* Vol. 4 No. 1 (1994): 6-10.

14. The Confederates withdrew from Kentucky through the Cumberland Gap into Tennessee. Kenneth A. Hafendorfer, *Perryville: Battle for Kentucky*, 2nd ed. (Louisville, KY: KH Press, 1991), 438-440.

15. Brig. Gen. John Porter McCown.

16. Brigadier General Green Clay Smith. He had defeated John Hunt Morgan at the battle of Lebanon, Tennessee in May 1862. Ezra J. Warner, *Generals in Blue: Lives of the Union Commanders* (Baton Rouge: Louisiana State University Press, 194), 457; and Hafendorfer, *They Died by Twos and Tens*, 56-58.

17. Abraham Buford sided with the Confederacy only in 1862 when Smith and Bragg entered the state. That, combined with the fact that two of his cousins were at this time Union generals, likely contributed to the idea that he was a poor choice to recruit Kentuckians for the Confederate cause. Warner, *Generals in Gray*, 39.

18. Major George Washington Morgan, familiarly known as "Major Wash," suffered a mortal wound to the neck. He appears to have been a collateral relative of John Hunt Morgan. Basil W. Duke, *History of Morgan's Cavalry* (Cincinnati: Miami Printing and Publishing Company, 1867), 170, 286; and *A Union Woman in Civil War Kentucky: The Diary of Frances Peter*, edited John David Smith and William Cooper, Jr. (Lexington: University Press of Kentucky, 2000), 66.

19. Colonel John Hunt Morgan's command surprised a Union brigade at Hartsville, Tennessee, on December 7, 1862. While Tucker's numbers are exaggerated, Morgan's men had achieved an overwhelming victory. They took 1,800 prisoners, 2,000 firearms, a two artillery pieces. The

success of this raid would result in Morgan's long-awaited promotion to general. *OR* 20(1):62; and Duke, *A History of Morgan's Cavalry*, 308-317.

20. Likely because they saw Pegram as an outsider; his early war service had been ignominious and followed by several staff positions, lately as chief of staff for Edmund Kirby Smith during the Kentucky Campaign. As Tucker's letter of November 12 indicates, the cavalrymen did welcome an infantry general appointed to command them. Griggs, *General John Pegram*, 56-57.

Chapter 8

1. John Pegram, Military Leaders Files, "13 March 1863 Affidavit, Valuations of Staff Horses," Eleanor S. Brockenbrough Library, Museum of the Confederacy, Richmond, Virginia.

2. Hess, *The Civil War in the West*, 126-133; and Griggs, *General John Pegram*, 63-65.

3. Report of Brig. Gen. John Pegram, C.S. Army, commanding expedition, April 1, 1863, in *OR* 23(1):171.

4. Report of Brig. Gen. John Pegram, C.S. Army, commanding expedition, April 1, 1863, in *OR* 23(1):172

5. Report of Brig. Gen. John Pegram, C.S. Army, commanding expedition, April 1, 1863, in *OR* 23(1):173.

6. Griggs, *General John Pegram*, 68-75.

7. David A. Powell, *Failure in the Saddle: Nathan Bedford Forrest, Joseph Wheeler, and the Confederate Cavalry in the Chickamauga Campaign* (New York: Savas Beatie, 2010), 225, 226.

8. Tucker Randolph Papers, MC-3 Collection, Eleanor S. Brockenbrough Library, Museum of the Confederacy, Richmond, Virginia.

9. Brig. Gen. Henry Davidson.

10. Col. John T. Wilder received permission to mount his infantry brigade in February 1863. Wilder also armed it with Spencer repeating rifles; due to its speed and firepower, it became known as the "Lightning Brigade" after its successful fight at Hoover's Gap on June 24, 1863. Glenn W. Sunderland, *Lightning at Hoover's Gap: Wilder's Brigade in the Civil War* (New York: Thomas Yoseloff, 1969), 25-43.

11. Daniel's account concludes as follows:

"Soon afterwards, when these & other eminent services wld have received recognition by promotion and confirmation in his command of the Division, Genl Pegram received his transfer to Virginia, for which he had petitioned time & again. Rather than seem fickle & capricious, he accepted it without a murmur & at once came to Virginia where he was assigned to command the gallant old Fourth Brigade of the A.N.V. in Dec 1863. Having no legal status in the Army of Tennessee, Tucker Randolph returned with his beloved commander to his native state (for which they had both pined) as volunteer aide-de-camp, acting as such in the Mine Run affair, when Genl Meade made a demonstration across the Rapid Ann in the depth of that winter.

"In the same capacity he participated in all the engagements of the Fourth Brigade in the campaign of the Army of Northern Virginia in the Spring of 1864, until the memorable battle of 'Second Cold Harbor,' where he yielded up his young life in the desperate charge that decimated his brigade.

"Such is an imperfect summary of the military career of Tucker Randolph, so distinguished for personal courage, military capacity, & patriotic devotion as to excite the enthusiastic admiration of his comrades, while his just and affectionate nature, his manly bearing & Christian character endeared him to all his associates."

12. Griggs, *General John Pegram*, 86-87.

Chapter 9

1. Ambrose P. Hill's men left their camps early, at around 5 a.m., while Ewell made a later start. Ewell's men faced difficulty in the early stages of the march because Hill's men clogged the roads. William D. Henderson, *The Road to Bristoe Station: Campaigning with Lee and Meade, August 1–October 20, 1863* (Lynchburg, VA: H. E. Howard, 1987), 84.

2. J.E.B. Stuart and the Confederate cavalry had opened the way for Lee's infantry to move against the Army of the Potomac. On October 10, Stuart's men had moved out and the following day fought a large engagement at Brandy Station. A modern estimate pegs Union losses at 400, overall, for the fighting of October 11. Henderson, *Road to Bristoe Station*, 87-103.

3. Ewell's corps moved against the Union troops near Auburn. Jubal Early's division swung to the west to flank the Federals, and as Tucker describes, they encountered little opposition. Henderson, *Road to Bristoe Station*, 150-162.

4. Lieutenant General Ambrose Powell Hill committed two brigades recklessly, with reserves and reinforcements too far away to be of use. Consequently, much as Tucker states, the Confederates faced long odds. After the battle, Lee criticized Hill about the Battle of Bristoe Station. Henderson, *Road to Bristoe Station*, 170, 192-193.

5. Brigadier General William W. Kirkland and Brigadier General John R. Cooke were wounded in the leg and arm, respectively. Shell splinters

wounded Brigadier General Carnot Posey in the late afternoon. He would die from his wounds in a hospital. Earl J. Hess, *Lee's Tar Heels: The Pettigrew-Kirkland-MacRae Brigade* (Chapel Hill: University of North Carolina Press, 2002), 190; and Henderson, *Road to Bristoe Station*, 189.

6. Presumably Tucker means either North Carolina brigade of Brigadier General William W. Kirkland or Brigadier General John R. Cooke. Both brigades, sent on an ill-considered attack, ran into heavy Union opposition. During the fighting, Kirkland's brigade, by a modern estimate, took about 40% losses, hardly "running before some Yankee skirmishers." Cooke's brigade took 27% losses, better only by comparison with Kirkland's brigade. A soldier in Cooke's brigade professed "we suffered very severely. It was the hottest place I ever saw. Sharpsburg was not near so hot." When the Confederate infantry fell back, they left exposed 5 guns of Major David G. McIntosh's Battalion. Union infantry proceeded to haul them off by hand ropes. H. M. Wagstaff, editor, "The James A. Graham Papers, 1861-1884," *James Sprunt Historical Studies* Vol. 20, No. 2:157; Hess, *Lee's Tar Heels*, 184-192; Henderson, *Road to Bristoe Station*, 185, 189.

7. Raleigh Travers Daniel, Jr., who had been appointed Pegram's assistant adjutant general in November 1862. Krick, *Staff Officers in Gray*, 109.

8. Nathaniel Beverley Tucker, born in Winchester in 1820, had been a journalist and printer. He had been appointed a consul in London in 1857, and the outbreak of the war found him there. He subsequently served as Confederate agent in England and France in 1862. During 1863 and 1864 he procured supplies for the Confederacy in Canada, and Tucker Randolph likely alludes to one of these forays (his other uncle, Captain John Randolph Tucker, commanded the Charleston Squadron at this time). Lyon Gardiner Tyler, editor, *Encyclopedia of Virginia Biography*, Vol. III (New York: Lewis Historical Publishing Company, 1915), 145; and Werlich, *Admiral of the Amazon*, 53-60.

9. Major Ambrose Robert Hite Ranson, Pegram's commissary of subsistence, had left Pegram's staff in October 1863, before being appointed an ordnance officer under Lieutenant Colonel Briscoe Baldwin of Lee's headquarters staff at the end of December. A. R. H. Ranson, "Reminiscences of the Civil War by a Confederate Staff Officer (Fourth Paper)," *The Sewanee Review* Vol. 22 No. 3 (July 1914): 305-306; and Krick, *Staff Officers in Gray*, 250.

10. John Pegram's mother, Virginia Pegram, lived in a home on Linden Row on Franklin Street in Richmond. Griggs, *General John Pegram*, 93.

11. Raleigh Travers Daniel's father Raleigh Travers Daniel, Sr., lived in Richmond.

12. Uncle John Randolph Tucker.

13. Richmond publisher West and Johnston issued from 1863 to 1864 a translation of Victor Hugo's *Les Misérables*. *Jean Valjean* was the final of five parts, the others being *Fantine, Cosette, Marius*, and *St. Denis*. The first American translation had appeared in New York in 1862; the Richmond translation omitted some passages that would be offensive to the South and also excised considerable portions of the text due to scarce resources. Richard Harwell, *The Confederate Hundred: A Bibliophilic Selection of Confederate Books* (Urbana, Illinois: Beta Phi Mu, 1964), 25; and Olin Moore, "Some Translations of *Les Misérables*," *Modern Language Notes* Vol. 74, No. 3(March 1959), 240-246.

14. On February 5, 1864 Union general-in-chief Henry Wager Halleck ordered the Army of the Potomac, under the temporary command of Major General John Sedgwick in the absence of Major General George G. Meade, to demonstrate against Confederate forces. In so doing, Halleck hoped the Army of the Potomac would prevent Lee from sending troops to Tidewater, Virginia, where Major General Benjamin F. Butler planned to embark on an expedition. The following day, February 6, Union cavalry demonstrated at several fords along the

Rapidan, while the infantry of the Second Corps drew Confederate attention near Morton's Ford. Martin F. Graham and George F. Skoch, *Mine Run: A Campaign of Lost Opportunities: October 21, 1863-May 1, 1864* (Lynchburg, VA: H. E. Howard, 1987), 85-87.

15. Elements of the 3rd Division of the Union Second Corps crossed the Rapidan River to take Confederate rifle pits, despite having been ordered to stay on the northern bank. Graham and Skoch, *Mine Run*, 88.

16. After driving Confederate skirmishers away, the Union troops had proceeded to push forward to the Morton homestead. Graham and Skoch, *Mine Run*, 88.

17. Lieutenant R. M. Anderson commanded the 1st Company, Richmond Howitzers. His commander praised "the gallantry, promptness, and constancy" of the artillerists, noting that "without support, they drove back the enemy and held them in check until the arrival of infantry support." *OR* 33:142.

18. Brigadier General John Brown Gordon commanded a brigade composed entirely of Georgia regiments but was away from the army. His absence left Colonel Clement Anselm Evans in charge of his brigade. On the morning of the 6th, Lieutenant General Richard S. Ewell sent for Evans's brigade, and as it embarked on the march to Morton's Ford, a courier informed Evans that he had command of the Division. Robert Grier Stephens, Jr., *Intrepid Warrior: Clement Anselm Evans, Confederate General from Georgia: Life, Letters, and Diaries of the War Years* (Dayton, OH: Morningside, 1992), 348.

19. Colonel John S. Hoffman of the 31st Virginia Infantry Regiment commanded Pegram's brigade. He was "distinguished for his great physique, his bachelorhood and his fondness for a game or euchre or whist." Stephens, *Intrepid Warrior*, 350; and Krick, *Lee's Colonels*, 194.

20. Brigadier General Stephen Dodson Ramseur commanded a North Carolina brigade in Early's Division; it had been stationed on picket duty at Morton's Ford. Ramseur himself almost fell into Union hands; he complained to his brother, "I made a narrow escape, riding into the Yanks without warning from our worthless Art'y." George G. Kundahl, editor, *The Bravest of the Brave: The Correspondence of Stephen Dodson Ramseur* (Chapel Hill: University of North Carolina Press, 2010), 197-198.

21. Captain Buckner MaGill Randolph of Company C of the 49th Virginia Infantry Regiment. Laura Virginia Hale and Stanley S. Phillips, *History of the Forty-ninth Virginia Infantry C.S.A: "Extra Billy Smith's Boys"* (Lanham, MD: S.S. Phillips and Assc., 1981), 234.

22. The 3rd Division of the Second Corps, according to a modern estimate, lost 11 killed, 204 wounded, and 40 captured or missing. Graham and Skoch, *Mine Run*, 94.

23. Major General Winfield Scott Hancock usually commanded the Second Corps but remained absent, recovering from a wound suffered at Gettysburg. Instead, Major General Gouverneur K. Warren had command of the Union Second Corps. On February 7, Warren felt ill and turned the command over to Brigadier General John C. Caldwell. But, after the heavy fighting during the day, Warren resumed command at around 3:00 p.m. Graham and Skoch, *Mine Run*, 87, 89.

24. Confederate losses tallied 4 killed, 20 wounded, and at least 25 missing. Graham and Skoch, *Mine Run*, 94.

25. The Union cavalry demonstrated at Barnett's Ford, and, unlike Warren's men, remained on the north side of the Rapidan. Graham and Skoch, *Mine Run*, 87.

26. S. H. Goetzel of Mobile, Alabama, printed a Confederate edition of George Eliot's *Silas Marner: The Weaver of Raveloe* in 1863. T. Michael Parrish and Robert M. Willingham, Jr., *Confederate Imprints:*

A Bibliography of Southern Publications from Secession to Surrender (Austin, TX: Jenkins Publishing Co, n.d.), 540-541.

27. A standard pharmacological text of the 19th century stated that "arsenic acid (formerly termed white arsenic) and its solution with potash (Liq. Potassae Arsenitis)…are principally used in obstinate chronic diseases of the skin." Henry Beasley, *The Book of Prescriptions* (Philadelphia: Lindsay & Blakiston, 1855), 81.

28. Colonel James Jackson Morrison, colonel of the 1st Georgia Cavalry Regiment, temporarily commanded Pegram's former brigade, though the composition had shifted slightly. Morrison resigned on grounds of poor health in April 1864. Stewart Sifakis, *Compendium of the Confederate Armies: South Carolina and Georgia* (New York: Facts on File, 1995), 148; and Krick, *Lee's Colonels*, 283.

29. A hotel on the southern corner of the intersection of Franklin and Fourteenth Streets. Thomas, *Confederate State of Richmond*, 22.

30. Clark's Mountain provided Confederates a good vantage point to keep watch on the Army of the Potomac. Lee's assistant adjutant general, Walter Taylor, wrote in a letter: "There is a prominent point…from which we have the grandest view of the Blue Ridge and surrounding country for miles that I ever beheld. All the camps of enemy too are exposed to our view--just below us as it were." R. Lockwood Tower, editor, with John S. Belmont, *Lee's Adjutant: The Wartime Letters of Colonel Walter Herron Taylor, 1862-1865* (Columbia: University of South Carolina Press, 1995), 90.

31. On February 28, a major Union cavalry raid under the command of Brigadier General Judson Kilpatrick, with a column under the command of Colonel Ulric Dahlgren, set out to attack Richmond and free prisoners of war held there. A scratch Confederate force kept the raiders at bay in the outskirts of the city. On 3 March, Confederate defenders killed Dahlgren in action in King and Queen County, and upon examining his corpse, found papers that indicated he would try

burn Richmond as well as kill or capture Jefferson Davis and other Confederate officials. Questions about the authenticity of those papers persist to this day, but Confederates at the time saw little reason to doubt their veracity, and viewed them as an affront to the rules of war. Bruce M. Venter, *Kill Jeff Davis: The Union Raid on Richmond, 1864* (Norman: University of Oklahoma Press, 2016), 265-278 and *passim*.

32. "Miss Cary" is Hetty Cary, a secessionist from Baltimore who had relocated to Richmond after the start of the Civil War. Her sister, Jennie, arranged the music for the poem "My Maryland," which resulted in the popular Southern air "Maryland! My Maryland!" The Cary sisters, along with their cousin Constance, created quite the splash on the social scene in Richmond, meeting and dining with Confederate dignitaries. At the behest of the Confederate Congress, they sewed the first three Confederate battle flags. John Pegram met Hetty Cary on the Richmond social scene in early 1862 when both were in the city. Pegram went west to cavalry, while Hetty returned to Baltimore. Hetty remained there until mid-1863 and as related above, Pegram remained in the west until late summer 1863. Both in the vicinity of Richmond, they began to see each other on the social scene. The pair were married on January 19, 1865. Griggs, *General John Pegram*, 39-42, 46-48, 86-87, 92-93, 96-97, 114-15.

33. Kilpatrick's force indeed numbered 3,582 men. During the course of the raid it took 340 casualties and lost more than 600 horses. Venter, *Kill Jeff Davis*, 98, 249.

34. That is, the Kilpatrick-Dahlgren raid.

Chapter 10

1. The best description of these movements and battles is found in the volumes by Gordon C. Rhea. Gordon C. Rhea, *The Battle of the Wilderness, May 5-6, 1864* (Baton Rouge: Louisiana State University Press, 1994); and Gordon C. Rhea, *The Battles for Spotsylvania Court House and the Road to Yellow Tavern, May 7–12, 1864* (Baton Rouge: Louisiana State University Press, 1997). For the Battle of Spotsylvania, see also: William D. Matter, *If It Takes All Summer: The Battle of Spotsylvania* (Chapel Hill: University of North Carolina Press, 1988).

2. Tucker's letter written on May 23 implies that Tucker had accompanied Pegram to Richmond after Pegram suffered a wound at the Battle of Wilderness on May 5.

3. By May 10, Lee's army and Grant's army confronted each other near Spotsylvania Courthouse. Lee's troops had entrenched in a strong position, except for a salient that jutted northward. Richard S. Ewell's men held this salient; on the evening of 10 May, Union troops launched an attack. They enjoyed brief success and captured parts of the Confederate line, until fierce counterattacks drove them back. The momentary success on May 10 gave Union leadership the idea to launch a larger attack, which would come on May 12. Rhea, *The Battles for Spotsylvania Court House*, 166-180.

4. Lee's presence to bolster his troops demonstrated the faltering condition of the Army of Northern Virginia; earlier in the war, the matter could have been handled without the Army commander's direct intervention. An earlier, famous episode, had taken place on May 6, with Lee encouraging the Texas Brigade. Lee had already intervened on the field on May 10 near the salient. When Union troops overran the salient on May 12, the scale of the disaster necessitated closer intervention from the Confederate chief. Robert K. Krick, "'Lee to the Rear,' the Texans Cried," in *The Wilderness Campaign*, edited by Gary W. Gallagher (Chapel Hill: University of North Carolina Press, 1997), 160-200; Robert K. Krick, "An Insurmountable Barrier between the

Army and Ruin: The Confederate Experience at Spotsylvania's Bloody Angle," in *The Spotsylvania Campaign*, edited by Gary W. Gallagher (Chapel Hill: University of North Carolina Press, 1998), 80-126; and Rhea, *Battles for Spotsylvania Court House*, 232-307.

5. Captain Robert N. Wilson, Pegram's assistant adjutant general. Krick, *Staff Officers in Gray*, 306.

6. Pegram received a wound to the leg during the fighting at Wilderness on May 5 and travelled by ambulance to Richmond. Apparently, based on his letter, Tucker accompanied Pegram to Richmond and made his way back to brigade by the May 10. Griggs, *General John Pegram C.S.A.*, 96.

7. Lieutenant Colonel George Augustus Goodman. Though only in his mid-thirties during the Civil War, his men called him "Old Gus," "Aunt Sally," or "Old Granny." Krick, *Lee's Colonels*, 160.

8. Lieutenant General James Longstreet and Lieutenant General Ambrose Powell Hill commanded two of the three corps in Lee's Army of Northern Virginia at this time. Longstreet had been wounded during the battle of Wilderness, so Major General Richard H. Anderson commanded his corps. Rhea, *The Battles for Spotsylvania Court House*, 340.

9. Brigadier General Thomas Rosser commanded a brigade of Confederate cavalry. Millard Kessler Bushong and Dean McKoin Bushong, *Fightin' Tom Rosser, C.S.A.* (Shippensburg, PA: Beidel Printing House, 1983), 91-92.

10. Major General Charles W. Field led a division in Longstreet/ Anderson's Corps. Rhea, *The Battles for Spotsylvania Court House*, 340.

11. Major General Edward Johnson led a division in Lieutenant General Richard S. Ewell's corps. Rhea, *The Battles for Spotsylvania Court House*, 342.

12. Brigadier General Harry T. Hays led a brigade in Major General Jubal A. Early's division. Rhea, *The Battles for Spotsylvania Court House*, 342.

13. At this time, Jones's Brigade was led by Colonel William Witcher and Colonel Zebulon York commanded Stafford's Brigade. Both were in Johnson's Division. Rhea, *The Battles for Spotsylvania Court House*, 342.

14. Colonel James H. Skinner of the 52nd Virginia Infantry Regiment. Skinner had already been wounded twice before at Second Manassas and Gettysburg. In this battle, Skinner was hit "in the temple by a minie ball, ball entered just below the left temple passed through the left eye and made its exit on the right side of the nose just below the left corner of the right eye." He eventually regained sight in his right eye. Robert J. Driver, Jr., *52nd Virginia Infantry* (Lynchburg, VA: H. E. Howard, 1986), 150; and Krick, *Lee's Colonels*, 350.

15. Lieutenant Colonel John G. Kasey of the 58th Virginia Infantry Regiment suffered a wound to the hip. Robert J. Driver, Jr., *58th Virginia Infantry* (Lynchburg, VA: H. E. Howard, 1990), 115.

16. Major William Pope Cooper of the 31st Virginia Infantry Regiment received a wound to the left hip. John M. Ashcraft, *31st Virginia Infantry* (Lynchburg, VA: H. E. Howard, 1988), 122.

17. Major John Doak Lilley was hit "in the left arm, and leg, right hand lost two fingers." Driver, *52nd Virginia Infantry*, 130.

Chapter 11

1. C. B. Christian, "The Battle at Bethesda Church," *Southern Historical Society Papers*, Vol. 33 (Richmond: Southern Historical Society, 1905), 59-60.

2. Colonel Edward Willis of the 12th Georgia Infantry Regiment commanded Pegram's brigade at Bethesda Church. He died as a result of the fighting, being reported wounded and missing in action. Krick, *Lee's Colonels*, 405.

3. Lt. James Francis Madison "Frank" Ranson served as Pegram's aide-de-camp and was brother of Ambrose Robert Hite Ranson. Krick, *Staff Officers in Gray*, 250.

4. *Richmond Daily Dispatch*, June 1, 1864 and June 8, 1864.

Bibliography

Archival Sources

Library of Virginia
    1860 United States Census Microfilm
    1860 United States Census Slave Schedules Microfilm
    Henrico County Tax Records 1859 Microfilm
    Henrico County Tax Records 1860 Microfilm
    Samuel Bassett French Papers
        Biographical sketch of Norman Vincent Randolph
        Biographical sketch of Captain Tucker St. Joseph Randolph

Museum of the Confederacy, Eleanor S. Brockenbrough Library (now
in the collections of the Virginia Historical Society)
    MC-3, R-137 File
    Military Leaders File—John Pegram
    Tucker Randolph Papers

Private Collections
Janet Randolph Turpin Ayers
Photograph of St. Joseph Tucker Randolph and Norman
Vincent Randolph
Randolph Family Bible

Earl Gregg Swemm Library, College of William and Mary
Telegrams and Letters Received by the Confederate States War
Department, 273-L-1862

Virginia Historical Society
J. W. Randolph Papers

Newspapers

Richmond Daily Dispatch

Published Works

Allan, William. *History of the Campaign of Gen. T. J. (Stonewall) Jackson in the Shenandoah Valley of Virginia.* Philadelphia: J.B. Lippincott, 1880.

Allardice, Bruce S. *More Generals in Gray.* Baton Rouge: Louisiana State University Press, 1995.

Anderson, Paul Christopher. *Blood Image: Turner Ashby in the Civil War and the Southern Mind.* Baton Rouge: Louisiana State University Press, 2002.

Ashby, Thomas M. *Life of Turner Ashby.* New York: Neale Publishing, 1914.

Ashcraft, John M. *31st Virginia Infantry.* Lynchburg, VA: H. E. Howard, 1988.

Bearss, Ed. *River of Lost Opportunities: The Civil War on the James River 1861-1862.* Lynchburg, VA: H. E. Howard, 1995.

Beasley, Henry. *The Book of Prescriptions.* Philadelphia: Lindsay & Blakiston, 1855.

Bergeron, Arthur W. Jr. *Guide to Louisiana Confederate Military Units 1861–1865*. Baton Rouge: Louisiana State University Press, 1989.

Bridges, Peter. *Pen of Fire: John Moncure Daniel*. Kent, OH: Kent State University Press, 2002.

Brooke, George M. Jr., *Ironclads and Big Guns of the Confederacy: The Journal and Letters of John M. Brooke*. Columbia: University of South Carolina Press, 2002.

Buck, Irving A. *Cleburne and His Command*, edited by Thomas Robson Hay. Reprint, Jackson, TN: McCowat-Mercer Press, 1959 (1908).

Bushong, Millard Kessler and Dean McKoin Bushong. *Fightin' Tom Rosser, C.S.A.* Shippensburg, PA: Beidel Printing House, 1983.

Carmichael, Peter S. *The Last Generation: Young Virginians in Peace, War, and Reunion*. Chapel Hill: University of North Carolina Press, 2005.

——. *The Purcell, Crenshaw and Letcher Artillery*. Lynchburg, VA: H. E. Howard, 1990.

Chamberlayne, C. G. *Ham Chamberlayne-Virginian: Letters and Papers of an Artillery Officer in the War for Southern Independence 1861-1865*. Richmond, VA: Press of the Dietz Printing Co., 1932.

Christian, C. B. "The Battle at Bethesda Church." *Southern Historical Society Papers*, Vol. 33. Richmond: Southern Historical Society, 1905.

Clemmer, Gregg S. *Old Alleghany: The Life and Wars of General Ed Johnson*. Staunton, VA: Hearthside Publishing Company, 2004.

Confederate Military History. Confederate Publishing Company, 1899; reprint, Wilmington, NC: Broadfoot Publishing Company, 1987-88.

Crofts, Daniel W. *Reluctant Confederates: Upper South Unionists in the Secession Crisis*. Chapel Hill: University of North Carolina Press, 1989.

Curry, W. L. *Four Years in the Saddle: History of the First Regiment Ohio Volunteer Cavalry*. Columbus, OH: Champlin Printing Company, 1898.

Cutchins, John A. *A Famous Command: The Richmond Light Infantry Blues*. Richmond, VA: Garrett & Massie, 1934.

Daniels, Jonathan. *The Randolphs of Virginia*. Garden City, NY: Doubleday, 1972.

Driver, Robert J., Jr. *52nd Virginia Infantry*. Lynchburg, VA: H. E. Howard, 1986.

——. *58th Virginia Infantry*. Lynchburg, VA: H. E. Howard, 1990.

Dudley, William S. *Going South: U.S. Navy Officer Resignations and Dismissals on the Eve of the Civil War.* Washington, DC: Naval Historical Foundation, 1981.

Duke, Basil W. *History of Morgan's Cavalry.* Cincinnati: Miami Printing and Publishing Company, 186.

Ecelbarger, Gary L. *Frederick W. Lander: The Great Natural American Soldier.* Baton Rouge: Louisiana State University Press, 2000.

——. *"We are in for it!": The First Battle of Kernstown.* Shippensburg, PA: White Mane Publishing Company, 1997.

Edwards, William B. *Civil War Guns.* Harrisburg, PA: The Stackpole Company, 1962.

Elliott, Sam Davis., ed. *Doctor Quintard: Chaplain C.S.A. and Second Bishop of Tennessee: The Memoir and Civil War Diary of Charles Todd Quintard.* Baton Rouge: Louisiana State University Press, 2003.

Ferslew, Eugene W. *Second Annual Directory for the City of Richmond to Which is Added a Business Directory for 1860.* Richmond: Eugene W. Ferslew, 1860.

Freeman, Douglas Southall. *A Calendar of Confederate Papers with a Bibliography of Some Confederate Publications.* Richmond, VA: The Confederate Museum, 1908.

Gaines, William H., Jr.. *Biographical Register of Members: Virginia State Convention of 1861 First Session.* Richmond: State Library of Virginia 1969.

Goode, G. Brown. *Virginia Cousins: A Study of the Ancestry and Posterity of John Goode of Whitby, a Virginia Colonist of the Seventeenth Century, with Notes Upon Related Families, a Key to Southern Genealogy, and a History of the English Surname Gode, Goad, Goode or Good from 1148 to 1887.* Richmond, VA: J. W. Randolph & English, 1887.

Graham, Martin F. and George F. Skoch. *Mine Run: A Campaign of Lost Opportunities: October 21, 1863-May 1, 1864.* Lynchburg, VA: H. E. Howard, 1987.

Griggs, Walter S., Jr. *General John Pegram C. S. A.* Lynchburg, VA: H. E. Howard, 1993.

Hafendorfer, Kenneth A. *The Battle of Richmond, Kentucky August 30, 1862.* Lousiville, KY: KH Press, 2006.

——. *Perryville: Battle for Kentucky,* 2nd Ed. Louisville, KY: KH Press, 1991.

——. *They Died by Twos and Tens: The Confederate Cavalry in the Kentucky Campaign of 1862*. Louisville, KY: KH Press, 1995.

Hale, Laura Virginia and Stanley S. Phillips. *History of the Forty-ninth Virginia Infantry C.S.A: "Extra Billy Smith's Boys"*. Lanham, MD: S.S. Phillips and Assc., 1981.

Harrison, Fairfax. *The Virginia Carys: An Essay in Genealogy*. New York: De Vinne Press, 1919.

Harwell, Richard. *The Confederate Hundred: A Bibliophilic Selection of Confederate Books*. Urbana, Illinois: Beta Phi Mu, 1964.

Henderson, William D. *The Road to Bristoe Station: Campaigning with Lee and Meade, August 1-October 20, 1863*. Lynchburg, VA: H. E. Howard, 1987.

Hess, Earl J. *The Civil War in the West: Victory and Defeat from the Appalachians to the Mississippi*. Chapel Hill: University of North Carolina Press, 2012.

——. *Lee's Tar Heels: The Pettigrew-Kirkland-MacRae Brigade*. Chapel Hill: University of North Carolina Press, 2002.

Hotchkiss, Jedediah. *Confederate Military History: Volume IV: Virginia*. Reprint; Wilmington, NC: Broadfoot Publishing Company, 1987 [1899].

Howard, McHenry. *Recollections of a Maryland Confederate Soldier and Staff Officer Under Johnston, Jackson and Lee*. Baltimore: Williams & Wilkins, 1914.

Hughes, Nathaniel Cheairs, Jr., and Gordon D. Whitney. *Jefferson Davis in Blue: The Life of Sherman's Relentless Warrior*. Baton Rouge: Louisiana State University Press, 2002.

Jordan, Ervin L., Jr. *Black Confederates and Afro-Yankees in Civil War Virginia*. Charlottesville: University Press of Virginia, 1995.

Kimball, Gregg D. *American City, Southern Place: A Cultural History of Antebellum Richmond*. Athens: University of Georgia Press, 2000.

Krick, Robert E. L. *Staff Officers in Gray: A Biographical Register of the Staff Officers in the Army of Northern Virginia*. Chapel Hill: University of North Carolina Press, 2003.

Krick, Robert K. *The Fredericksburg Artillery*. Lynchburg, VA: H. E. Howard, 1986.

——. "An Insurmountable Barrier between the Army and Ruin: The Confederate Experience at Spotsylvania's Bloody Angle," in *The*

Spotsylvania Campaign, edited by Gary W. Gallagher. Chapel Hill: University of North Carolina Press, 1998.

——. *Lee's Colonels: A Biographical Register of the Field Officers of the Army of Northern Virginia.* 5th Ed., Rev. Wilmington, NC: Broadfoot Publishing Company, 2009.

——. "'Lee to the Rear,' the Texans Cried," in *The Wilderness Campaign,* edited by Gary W. Gallagher. Chapel Hill: University of North Carolina Press, 1997.

Kundahl, George G. editor. *The Bravest of the Brave: The Correspondence of Stephen Dodson Ramseur.* Chapel Hill: University of North Carolina Press, 2010.

Lamers, William M. *The Edge of Glory: A Biography of General William S. Rosecrans, U.S.A.* New York: Harcourt, Brace & World, 1961.

Lang, Theodore F. *Loyal West Virginia from 1861 to 1865.* Baltimore: The Deutsch Publishing Company, 1895.

Loehr, Charles T. *History of the Old First Virginia Infantry Regiment, Army of Northern Virginia.* Richmond: Wm. Ellis Jones, 1884.

Manarin, Louis H. and Lee A. Wallace, Jr., *Richmond Volunteers: The Volunteer Companies of the City of Richmond and Henrico County, Virginia 1861–1865.* Richmond, VA: Westover Press, 1969.

Mohon, James L. "Defending the Confederate Heartland: Company F of Henry Ashby's 2nd Tennessee Cavalry," *Civil War Regiments: A Journal of the American Civil War,* Vol. 4, No. 1 (1994): 1-43.

Moore, Albert Burton. *Conscription and Conflict in the Confederacy.* New York: Macmillan, 1924.

Moore, Olin. "Some Translations of Les Misérables," *Modern Language Notes* Vol. 74, No. 3 (March 1959), 240-246.

Morgan, William James, et. al., eds. *Autobiography of Charles Wilkes, U.S. Navy 1798-1877.* Washington, DC: Naval History Division, 1978.

Morrison, James L., Jr., editor. *The Memoirs of Henry Heth.* Westport, CT: Greenwood Press, 1974.

Nason, George W. *Minute Men of '61 who Responded to the First Call of President Abraham Lincoln...: History and Complete Roster of the Massachusetts Regiments.* Boston: Smith & McCance, 1910.

Parks, Joseph H. *General E. Kirby Smith C.S.A.* Baton Rouge: Louisiana State University Press, 1954.

Parrish, T. Michael and Robert M. Willingham, Jr. *Confederate Imprints: A Bibliography of Southern Publications from Secession to Surrender.* Austin, TX: Jenkins Publishing Co, n.d.

Powell, David A. *Failure in the Saddle: Nathan Bedford Forrest, Joseph Wheeler, and the Confederate Cavalry in the Chickamauga Campaign.* New York: Savas Beatie, 2010.

Rankin, Thomas M. *Stonewall Jackson's Romney Campaign January 1-February 20, 1862.* Lynchburg, VA: H.E. Howard, 1994.

Ranson, A. R. H. "Reminiscences of the Civil War by a Confederate Staff Officer (Fourth Paper)," *The Sewanee Review* Vol. 22 No. 3 (July 1914): 298-318.

Register of Officers of the Confederate States Navy 1861-1865, rev. ed. Washington, D.C.: Government Printing Office, 1931.

Reidenbaugh, Lowell. *Jackson's Valley Campaign: The Battle of Kernstown.* Lynchburg, VA: H. E. Howard, 1996.

Rhea, Gordon C. *The Battles for Spotsylvania Court House and the Road to Yellow Tavern May 7–12, 1864.* Baton Rouge: Louisiana State University Press, 1997.

Ridley, Bromfield L. *Battles and Sketches of the Army of Tennessee.* Mexico, MO: Missouri Printing & Publishing Co., 1906.

Riggs, Susan A. *21st Virginia Infantry.* Lynchburg, VA: H. E. Howard, 1991

Robertson, James I., Jr. *Stonewall Jackson: The Man, the Soldier, the Legend.* New York: MacMillan Publishing, 1997.

Sauers, Richard A. *The Devastating Hand of War: Romney, West Virginia, During the Civil War.* Shepherd College: The George Tyler Moore Center for the Study of the Civil War, 2000.

Scarborough, William Kauffman, ed. *The Diary of Edmund Ruffin: Volume 1: Toward Independence, October 1856–April 1861.* Baton Rouge: Louisiana State University Press, 1972.

Shively, Kathryn. *Nature's Civil War: Common Soldiers and the Environment in 1862 Virginia.* Chapel Hill: University of North Carolina Press, 2013.

Sifakis, Stewart. *Compendium of the Confederate Armies: South Carolina and Georgia.* New York: Facts on File, 1995.

Smith, John David and William Cooper, Jr., editors. *A Union Woman in Civil War Kentucky: The Diary of Frances Peter.* Lexington: University Press of Kentucky, 2000.

Stephens, Robert Grier, Jr. *Intrepid Warrior: Clement Anselm Evans, Confederate General from Georgia: Life, Letters, and Diaries of the War Years.* Dayton, OH: Morningside, 1992.

Strohm, Robert F. "J.W. Randolph, Bookman *Extraordinaire*," *Occasional Bulletin* of the Virginia Historical Society, No. 42 (June 1981): 7-8.

Strider, Robert Edward Lee. *The Life and Work of George William Peterkin.* Philadelphia: George W. Jacobs & Company, 1929.

Sunderland, Glenn W. *Lightning at Hoover's Gap: Wilder's Brigade in the Civil War.* New York: Thomas Yoseloff, 1969.

Thomas, Emory M. *The Confederate State of Richmond: A Biography of the Capital.* Austin: University of Texas Press.

Tower, R. Lockwood, editor, with John S. Belmont. *Lee's Adjutant: The Wartime Letters of Colonel Walter Herron Taylor, 1862-1865.* Columbia: University of South Carolina Press, 1995.

Tyler, Lyon Gardiner, editor. *Encyclopedia of Virginia Biography*, Vol. III. New York: Lewis Historical Publishing Company, 1915.

Venter, Bruce M. *Kill Jeff Davis: The Union Raid on Richmond, 1864.* Norman: University of Oklahoma Press, 2016.

Wagstaff, H.M. editor, "The James A. Graham Papers, 1861-1884," *James Sprunt Historical Studies*, Vol. 20, No. 2: 91-323.

Walker, Cornelius. *The Life and Correspondence of Rev. William Sparrow, D.D.* Philadelphia: James Hammond, 1876.

Wallace, Lee A. Jr. *A Guide to Virginia Military Organizations 1861-1865*, Rev. 2nd Ed. Lynchburg, VA: H. E. Howard, 1986.

Ward, Evelyn D. *The Children of Bladensfield.* New York: Viking Press, 1978.

Warner, Ezra. *Generals in Blue: Lives of the Union Commanders.* Baton Rouge: Louisiana State University Press, 1964.

——. *Generals in Gray: Lives of Confederate Commanders.* Baton Rouge: Louisiana State University Press, 1959.

—— and W. Buck Yearns. *Biographical Register of the Confederate Congress.* Baton Rouge: Louisiana State University Press, 1975.

The War of the Rebellion: A Compilation of the Official Records of the Union and Confederate Armies. 128 vols. Washington, DC: Government Printing Office, 1880-1901.

Werlich, David P. *Admiral of the Amazon: John Randolph Tucker, His Confederate Colleagues, and Peru*. Charlottesville: University Press of Virginia, 1990.

Wills, Mary Alice. *The Confederate Blockade of Washington, D.C. 1861-1862*. Parsons, WVA: McClain Printing Company, 1975.

Worsham, John. *One of Jackson's Foot Cavalry*, ed. James I. Robertson, Jr. Reprint. Jackson, TN: McCowat-Mercer Press, 1964 (1912).

Wright, Marcus J. *List of Staff Officers of the Confederate States Army*, with a new introduction by John M. Carroll. Reprint; Mattituck, NY: J.M. Carroll, 1983 [1891].

Index

About the Author

Peter C. Luebke received his PhD in history from the University of Virginia in 2014. He has extensive experience in the field of public history, including having worked as a historian for Virginia's historic highway marker program and as an editorial assistant for the scholarly online reference work Encyclopedia Virginia. Luebke has authored, coauthored, edited, or coedited multiple articles and books, including a scholarly edition of Albion Tourgée's *The Story of a Thousand* (2011).

35th Star Publishing
Charleston, West Virginia
www.35thstar.com

www.ingramcontent.com/pod-product-compliance
Lightning Source LLC
Chambersburg PA
CBHW060913120626
46553CB00001B/315